THE GOLD
IS IN THE RAINBOW

Financial Planning Through
the Life Cycle

Ron Southward
with Michael Kane

Published in 1998 by Stoddart Publishing Co. Limited
34 Lesmill Road, Toronto, Canada M3B 2T6
Tel. (416) 445-3333   Fax (416) 445-5967
Email customer.service@ccmailgw.genpub.com

02 01 00 99 98 1 2 3 4 5

Canadian Cataloguing in Publication Data

Southward, Ron
The gold is in the rainbow: financial planning through the life cycle

ISBN 0-7737-6011-3

1. Finance, Personal.   I. Kane, Michael, 1948–   .   II. Title

HG179.S532 1998   332.024   C98-931488-X

Cover Design: Angel Guerra
Text Design: Tannice Goddard
Typesetting: Kinetics Design & Illustration

Printed and bound in Canada

To my family:
those who preceded,
those who accompany,
and those who will follow

CONTENTS

—

Introduction   *vii*

White: In the Beginning   *1*

Purple: Passion and Pioneering   *15*

Green: Establishing Roots   *31*

Red: Ambition and Accomplishment   *53*

Gold: Free at Last   *105*

Silver: Contentment   *157*

Grey: With a Helping Hand   *179*

Summary   *187*

Index   *191*

INTRODUCTION

In the beginning, we are born. And as the economist John Kenneth Galbraith said, "In the long run, we are all dead." A lot can happen between these two points. What we come to know as life flashes by quicker than we realize. In what seems like the blink of an eye, we are looking back over the years. All too often we are not as pleased as we would like with the things we did or didn't do.

As we review the passing years, we'll find that things are more likely to happen the way we want if we have a clear vision of where we want to go. So, like a ship setting off to sea, we need to have an idea of our destination. Without that knowledge, we would drift aimlessly.

In navigation, maps, charts, and other equipment assist us in reaching our final port. There are methods to do the same with our lives. These include goal setting, planning, record keeping, adjusting, and reassessing. Unfortunately, most people do not like doing these tasks.

Life is complicated. We see things differently as we age. Goals change. People change. Heck, the whole world changes. This makes long-range planning, if we try to do it all at once, almost impossible. It is easier to do if we break it down into smaller pieces.

This book divides life into seven stages, but there is no set time limit for each stage. It will vary from person to person. Most often people move forward through the stages. On occasion, some people go backwards. And just when you think you have it all figured out, life provides a surprise that changes the whole game. You may not like all these surprises, but you will be amazed at how much they can teach you.

Life planning is not a science. Planning your own life is important, but keep it in perspective. The sun will continue to rise in the east regardless of your plans. You won't take yourself too seriously if you remember the words of psychologist R. D. Laing: "Life is a sexually transmitted disease, with one hundred percent mortality." Relax and have fun with your plans. Go ahead and dream. I encourage you to keep Helen Keller's conclusion in mind when making your plans: "Life is either a daring adventure or nothing at all."

Every plan must be built with an understanding that it may have to be changed. Always write your goals down in pencil. That way, you can change them easily. The captain of a ship knows he has to make corrections and adjustments along the way based on weather, winds, currents, and tides. He knows these things will vary his plan even before he leaves the harbour, but he still makes a series of plans: one to get out of the harbour, another to get out to the high seas, one for the high seas in calm conditions, one for the high seas in stormy conditions, and a whole other set of plans for arriving at the harbour of his choice.

Do you think our life is any different? I don't. So let's get started.

I give each of the seven stages of life — starting with birth — a simple title, a colour that I believe has a symbolic association with that particular stage.

Stage one is White. As in art, we all start with a blank canvas when we begin to build our life. The foundation of skills, knowledge, and habits for our life are put in place here.

Stage two starts in high school, though the beginning and duration of this stage can vary markedly for each individual. This is normally a time of passion. Passion of the intellect, the passion of adventure, and, of course, the passion of the heart. What better colour to symbolize the passion of this period than Purple?

The next stage focuses on establishing oneself in the matters of career, family, and community. Our lives take on a direction. We begin to establish roots. We grow. I have chosen to symbolize this stage with the colour Green.

The next stage is synonymous with achievement. We attain satisfaction in the pursuit of our full potential. "Get it while you are hot, baby, 'cause you are cold for a long, long time." This stage, when you are hot, when you are on top, is symbolized by the colour Red.

There are three more stages in what I call my Rainbow of Life. One hundred years ago, life expectancy was much shorter. In those days there would have been only one more step. But medical science keeps moving the bar. At the same time, human attitudes and expectations about life are changing rapidly. I believe we can now see three senior levels.

The first is a stage of freedom, to live life your own way. Thank you, Frank Sinatra. This is your time. The choices people make at this level will be all over the map but your choices will be made on your terms. What better colour to symbolize this period than the colour Gold?

All good things come to an end. However, today's youth-oriented culture would rather not "go quietly into that good night." This leaves the next senior stage as one that may not be quite as active. The word contentment summarizes it. I have chosen to symbolize it with the colour Silver.

We have now reached that final stage. It is a stage that is more passive and more focused on security. It is a return to dependence. I symbolize it with the colour Grey.

Each of the seven stages has a different focus. Each requires different plans. At each stage we must deal with educational, career, health, family, personal, and financial issues.

At each stage you will ask yourself the same simple questions. What do I want to do? Where do I want to do it? With whom do I want to share it? How can I maintain my health? What am I doing with my money? The answers will change, and they are never simple.

A person in the Purple stage of life may answer these questions very differently than someone in the Gold stage. So how do we prepare for the answers at each stage?

It is not always easy to plan each stage looking forward. Sometimes it may be easier if you start by trying to see your life from the other end first. I refer to this as rear-view mirror planning. An understanding of the different stages of life makes this type of planning easier. You will realize that some opportunities must be seized now and others can be left for another day.

Begin by imagining yourself as a secure senior in your nineties sharing your life's journey with a great-grandchild. Make your plans now so that you can enjoy telling your life story as much as others will enjoy listening.

Let's head out and talk about the journey.

WHITE

IN THE BEGINNING

—

"You've got to be kidding. I've just been born. I have no interest in thinking about life cycle or financial planning. I'm focusing on how to get fed, how to walk, how to talk. Others have suggested potty training is important. Go talk to my parents. This whole thing was their idea anyway."

Well, parents, there you have it. Sounds like this is your show. It all starts out that way. The challenge for parents is to help their children develop their own sense of responsibility during the years in White. The early years of a child's life are critically important. Children will likely learn more in their first dozen years than they will in the rest of their lives. You, dear parents, are the ones from whom they are going to learn most in those years.

The good news is that you have a bit of time before your children need to deal with money matters. However, the bad news is they will be watching what you do. You are their example, so I encourage you to remember the cardinal rule of all parenting: Your actions speak so loudly your kids can't hear what you're saying.

White will last from birth till somewhere in the teenage years. The stage starts with the child totally dependent and ends with a declaration of independence. Their declaration often arrives earlier than you expect, though their actions suggest they are not ready for the responsibilities that come with their statement. A parent may even think it a revolution. Your kids' actions will also speak so loudly you may not be able to hear what they are saying. Hang in there — this too shall pass.

It is very important to know what you are trying to instill in your children. Your goals should be clear. First, try to create an environment that exposes your children to a variety of experiences and education. Next, provide your children with encouragement as they discover their own talents. Finally, and most importantly, love them and help them to develop self-confidence.

All of this support ultimately leads to the day when they can be fully self-reliant. You can't protect your children from the world. All you can do is prepare them so that when the world challenges them, they have a foundation on which they can make their own choices. An entire life will be built around the skills and knowledge they acquire in White.

MONEY

Your child will learn many skills in the White stage of life. One of those skills will be how to relate to and manage money, an ability that is becoming of greater importance in our materialistic society. Just like every other skill, you will have the most responsibility to provide guidance in this area.

Before children leave the White stage, they will have developed their own money habits and attitudes. They will get most of these habits and attitudes from you, the ones you passed on with your actions rather than your speeches.

The good news is that you have the first three to five years of a child's life to get your own financial house in order. It's a good idea to implement now some of the suggestions we make in other stages such as Purple, Green, and Red. By doing so, you can ensure your example will be the one you intended.

EDUCATION FUNDS

You can involve your child in setting up an education fund. He or she will take a personal interest in watching it grow and at the same time learn some valuable lessons. The experience will ultimately benefit your child and act as an excellent example of your money management skills and your belief in your child's abilities. The cost of contributions may seem prohibitive but remember that you or your child will have to pay at some point. The predicted cost of four years at university in the year 2015 is $67,000. One way to prepare for this expense is by making regular contributions of just $100 a month for the next eighteen years. At 8% growth these payments will accumulate to $40,000 in eighteen years.

There are three common ways to set up an education fund. The simplest method uses a growth-oriented mutual fund that is held in trust for the child. There are no limits to contributions or restrictions on how the funds are actually used. Choose a long-term growth fund because it generates mostly capital gains. Most of the income taxes on these gains are deferred and are taxed to the child, who will be in a lower tax bracket than the parent. Any dividend or interest income is taxable to the contributor when it is earned, but the capital gains will be taxed only when they are realized. Currently, 25% of capital gains are not taxed. In order to fully meet Revenue Canada's requirements, the trustee should be someone other than the contributor. Most often one spouse is the contributor and the other the

Q: How much does a $67,000 education cost?

a $143,000

b $67,000

c $21,600

d $10,500

A: All are correct!

a The cost if you borrow money and pay it back over several years

b The cost if you pay cash at the time of education

c The cost if you start now and save regularly until the student goes to university

d The cost if you invest a lump sum today

Based on eighteen years until university age.
Courtesy of Trimark Mutual Funds.

trustee. One potential drawback to an in-trust account is that it becomes the property of the child when he or she turns eighteen. Children can use the money as they please. They may or may not decide to use it for education.

The second method to save money for a child's education is a Registered Education Savings Plan (RESP). This will become the most popular way of saving for a child's education because of the new 20% matching grant proposed by the federal government. RESPs have contribution limits of $4,000 per year to a lifetime maximum of $42,000 per child. The 20% matching grant applies only to contributions up to $2,000 annually, but this can provide a grant of up to $400 per year for each child. Unlike a Registered Retirement Savings Plan (RRSP), the contributions are not deductible at time of contribution, so a parent, grandparent, or doting aunt would be investing after-tax dollars. As with an RRSP, the annual income is not taxed, a policy that greatly increases the effect of compound interest as earnings are reinvested without Revenue Canada skimming the profits. Only the investment growth, not the principal, is taxed when received by the child. RESPs have some restrictions to ensure that the funds are used to support the educational needs of a beneficiary. However, new rules allow the transfer of the benefit to a different child or, under certain conditions, to the RRSP of the contributor. In addition, the companies sponsoring RESPs have their own rules to consider before you get into these programs.

The third option is to set up a life insurance policy for the child. This allows unlimited contributions, ongoing sheltering from income tax, and no time restrictions on when the policy is transferred to the child. It does, however, involve setting up a life insurance policy with the required medical and related costs. These programs have early surrender charges that make them unattractive in the short term.

All these programs lend themselves to a monthly or annual contribution program. Start one of these plans only if you are reasonably sure you can keep up the payments. If you bail out early, you will pay surrender charges, and you may even forfeit your contributions.

One underused resource in these matters is grandparents. One of Canada's leading mutual fund companies found that approximately 65% of seniors would consider contributing to their grandchildren's education. However, only one percent of grandparents are being asked. Do them a favour — ask. They don't know what to buy at Toys 'R' Us anyway. Their involvement could provide the basis for a very pleasant conversation each year with their grandchildren as they observe the progress of the fund.

CHILDREN AND MONEY

Kids start to grasp the concept of money around the age of three. This is when your teaching job begins. Introduce the concept of money through games and activities that use actual coins. Kids will quickly learn how many nickels are in a dime or how many quarters are in a dollar. Ask them to figure out how they can get 55 cents with only three coins. How about with seven coins? They can graduate to setting up their own little grocery store in the basement, where they can make their own purchases and make the required change. In a store, give children the money to pay for treats and have the clerk give the change to the child. Then the child accounts for the transaction to you.

The number of games and activities you can devise is limitless. Money bingo is one example. Make up a bingo card with a monetary amount in each square. Players find items in the newspaper, flyers, or catalogues that add up to the amount in each square. They cut out the choices and glue them on to the card to create a bingo. This flexible game can be done as a race among players or by a child alone.

Your child's interest is likely to increase if you use real money in games and activities. The game of Monopoly is another old standby that teaches about value and risk. It doesn't take a kid long to figure out the value of a hotel on Boardwalk.

Many books available deal with kids and money. Ask for some suggestions in the children's education section of your bookstore. Libraries also have some great material, and the Internet has sites where kids can learn about money matters.

ALLOWANCES

An allowance for a child is one of those topics for which there are more opinions than people. So I will give you my opinion.

Let me start by making a few of my own assumptions:

- The ultimate goal is to teach the child to manage his or her own money.
- You would be spending the money on the child anyway.
- Academic performance should not be tied to the allowance.
- Regular household chores should not be tied to the allowance. Just like adults, children should contribute to the smooth running of the household as best they can, without expecting payment. If extra jobs are assigned, payment may be negotiated.

You may have some different assumptions than these. But the important thing to remember is that if you do not train kids to handle their own money and have some ground rules established, you are heading for problems.

Children become very good at "tin cupping." This is what I call it when they are always asking you for money or things. They become adept at manipulating you and your spouse to get what they want. They play the two of you off each other. They seldom seem to appreciate the cost of things. And they never comparison shop to choose a less expensive item. They are constantly putting you in the position of the ogre or the cheapskate. All the kids ever hear from you is "No." Finally, children, like everyone else, are not particularly happy with any situation in which they are not in control. You may like being in control, but your goal is to transfer gradually financial responsibility to your children. Over time I believe you should try to transfer as many financial responsibilities to your children as possible. After all, they are going to have to face the real world sooner or later. Why not now, when you are there for guidance, and the risk and amounts are low?

How much to give as an allowance depends on your financial situation, what you expect the allowance to cover, and the child's age and capabilities. Experts seem to think that a child can grasp the concept of an allowance as early as age five, but you know your child best, so you will have to make your own call on that. The first step would be to give a small amount that the child could use to cover personal treats. Expand the amount to cover some entertainment costs as he or she starts to do things with friends independently of you. I always pay if the child is with me on a family outing.

Gradually, encourage your child to become responsible for his or her clothes purchases, haircuts, transportation, and most personal expenses as well. Increase the allowance as your child assumes these responsibilities. What may seem like a large allowance can actually save you money if it is providing all these things for the child.

The ideal position is when you no longer have to be the one to say "No." Your children will be spending their own money. It is surprising how much more astute their shopping skills become. The key is that you both know the allowance money is their money, and that it is a finite resource. Welcome to the real world.

Naturally, there is no such thing as an unbreakable rule. What are you going to do about special events — that school trip, a chance to go to a friend's cottage, or a special requirement for one of their activities? This is a judgment call. I feel that unique experiences provide great value, so I will make exceptions. These situations provide a good opportunity to discuss relative values, a topic I will talk about shortly.

From the beginning, be clear about the amount of the allowance and the child's responsibilities. Specify when you will pay the allowance and always pay on time. You do not want the child to have to ask for the money. It defeats the whole purpose. Remember, your example is the best teacher.

How you pay the allowance gives other opportunities to train children on the management of money. You can give them the money in three envelopes: one for personal expenses, one for sharing (gifts and charities), and one for saving. This will teach children to plan their expenditures more effectively and will allow them to learn how to save for a specific goal in the future. It will also establish the concept of sharing with others.

How long you pay an allowance will depend on your child's circumstances. He or she may be in school for years but a twenty-five-year-old grad student should not still be "tin cupping" by calling you up and asking for extra money. Either you are not providing a satisfactory base income or, unfortunately, he or she has not yet learned the basic lessons of financial management.

Now a topic which I regard to be quicksand — for both the parent and the child — giving advances or loans. I am not saying never to give them. However, they should truly be rare, as you are setting a very dangerous precedent and are defeating much of the good work you have done up till now. My own experience suggests loans to your children are most often regarded as forgivable loans. If that is the child's expectation, then the discussion should be about giving them the money, not lending the money. Ongoing gifts from you may create a system of family-supported welfare, for many of us have a different attitude to money that has not been earned. My father used a simple rule with me: if the bank will not lend you the money, and that is their business, why should he? That was not the message I wanted to hear at the time but I am the better for it today.

One of my father's favourite phrases was "value received." This is one of the great concepts you can pass on to your children, but you have formidable competition from every advertiser and business promotion, not to mention peer pressure. They are all yelling, Buy! Buy! Buy! Impulse buying and compulsive spending are the curse of our materialistic society.

Help your children to step back from this confusion and make their decisions based on their own needs and desires. They must analyze whether they will receive value from each purchase. This is another situation where your example speaks volumes. If you are an impulse buyer and all your credit cards are at the limit, what do you think your kids are learning? If you always buy the most expensive item, or the designer label, what do you think your kids will buy? If you are always desperate to get the next status symbol, what do you think your kids will want?

When your children subconsciously ask, "Do I need this?" or "Is it worth two weeks' allowance?", they can begin to measure value received in their own terms. Few skills are more worthy of a parent's encouragement than a child exercising good judgment. Remember, it is the child who has to make the decisions, not you.

I am not suggesting you create a bunch of penny pinchers. However, try to instill in them an ability to step back and judge value. Make a bit of a game out of analyzing advertisements, especially those that imply that if you use their product you can be popular or live happily ever after. Talk about how stores display their merchandise to maximize sales, so your children can resist the more obvious come-ons. Have your children do the math involved in some of your comparison shopping. Be careful to provide only guidance. The kids have to accept responsibility for their own money. Just remember the adage: "Good judgment comes from wisdom. Wisdom comes from experience. Experience comes from bad judgment." So give your kids some room. They have to get the experience.

Show your children how you track your own expenses. This is a great habit to learn early. If you have a computer, get a software program like Quicken that is easy to learn. In addition, banks are making their own software available. These tools will allow the kids to chart their own income and expenses. The financial picture that is produced will be worth a thousand words.

At various times, have philosophical discussions with children about the value of money in our lives. Ask them why the following expressions were developed and what their thoughts are about these statements.

- Money isn't everything.
- Easy come, easy go.
- It's made round, to go around.
- All you need is love.

Hopefully, you can develop an attitude in your children that money is a tool. It allows us to do things, have things, and give things. It can create satisfaction if handled effectively, or cause problems and stress if mismanaged. Money can be your master or you can master it. Your behaviour and habits will decide.

SAVINGS

Earlier, I opened up the topic of saving and talked about the three envelopes. It's not necessary to use envelopes to introduce the idea of budgeting and saving — it can start out with a piggy bank or anything else. The important thing is that some money is set aside for the future.

Once a child has a few dollars saved up, introduce him or her to the bank and start a savings account. This will give you a chance to explain what a bank does, what interest is, and what fees might be charged. Today, you can teach your children how to use the ATM and even track their account on the Internet.

Having a bank account is a big first step children take in developing a positive attitude to money management. Continuing to add money so that the account grows is the second big step. Deciding when and for what they will spend that money is the third.

The final step is learning that by just leaving the money there it can actually earn more money as interest. Compound interest is considered magic. It isn't, but does it ever do magical things! As your children begin to understand compound interest, introduce them to the Rule of 72. It is easy to use and can help in planning for their financial future. The Rule of 72 is this: You can tell how long it will take for an amount of money to double by dividing the interest rate into 72. As an example:

8% would divide into 72 a total of nine times. So the money would double in nine years.

Have your child check it out on a calculator. Key in 1,000 and multiply it by 1.08 (this is 8%) nine times. At the end of the nine calculations, the total will be close to 2,000. Of course, with eighteen calculations it will double twice to a total of 4,000. If a person left $1,000 untouched for 45 years, it would grow to $32,000 at an interest rate of 8%. Doesn't it seem to grow like magic?

The child soon understands that the higher the interest or growth rate is, the faster the money grows (e.g., at 12% it doubles in six years). With that knowledge, you can introduce them to a common stock or a mutual fund. If you started that education fund, you can use it as an example. The only way children will learn about stocks and mutual funds is if they have a personal stake. Helping them to buy stock of a company they are aware of (e.g., Coca-Cola, McDonald's) or a mutual fund is a great way to get them interested in opening the financial pages, if only to see how their own investments are doing.

LOOKING BACK

Well, your son or daughter is coming to the end of the White stage of life. Under your guidance, they have developed a strong sense of their own competencies and are confident to move on to take control of their personal and financial life. They are starting to think about getting jobs to earn their own money. They are starting to make decisions concerning their own activities without feeling they need your approval.

You'll never stop worrying about them. You'll never stop feeling you want to protect and guide them so they minimize the downside of "trial and error" learning. But, to a large extent, your period of great influence is over.

White was formative and learning. It is time to move to the period in your life when passion rules. Welcome to Purple.

PURPLE

PASSION AND PIONEERING

It is time to move on from pimples and puberty. It is now the time for passion and pioneering. You have arrived at Purple.

There is a saying that "youth is wasted on the young." Not for you. This is your time to start living your dream. In Purple, you are gaining your independence. However, it comes with the added burden of accepting full responsibility for yourself.

Experiences and responsibilities will come in several areas. You'll seize some opportunities but will pass by many others. And you will understand the challenge and consequences of making choices. The meaning of the words of Robert Frost's poem "The Road Not Taken" becomes more personal:

Yet knowing how way leads on to way,
I doubted if I should ever come back.

Decisions made in Purple will affect you forever. The first and most obvious are your decisions about education. It is in this period of your life that you acquire the basic knowledge for your lifetime's work. Initial experiences with work and business are established. Purple is the time when our physical strength peaks. The passion for adventure is at its pinnacle in Purple. Seize these opportunities when you can, because you may never again have the chance to experience these adventures. Also, in Purple you discover your feelings of sexuality and become a participant in the mating game. You have your first experience with romance.

How do you know when you arrive at Purple? There are several symptoms. You may get your first paying — although probably part-time — job. You may accept positions of leadership and responsibility. You have your first love. However, one almost infallible test is that you realize how dumb your parents have become. Cheer up. One of the tests to see when you are moving on to Green is whether you've discovered how much your parents seem to have learned while you were in Purple.

It is normal for people in the Purple stage to be fairly self-centred. Just remember while you are experiencing all these new things that your parents will be looking forward to the day when you are no longer financially dependent on them. After all, they are trying to move into Gold. So you had better make sure that you learn how to manage your own financial affairs as soon as possible. Trust me, your parents will be cheering you on. None of these experiences and skills can be isolated from each other. Decisions in one area affect decisions in another — if you go on to grad school, you may not be able to go to Australia, for example.

You will reach Purple while you are in high school, a time when you are starting to move your studies from the general to the more specific. Some people will have already realized that the world of academics is not for them. This is not a life-ending conclusion, but it does limit your choices significantly.

So before you make any decisions about what you will study

and what you won't, try to put into focus where you think you want to go in life. If you want to be a doctor, you will have to go to university. If your choice is auto mechanics, take advantage of opportunities available in high school. However, most young people have no idea of what they want to do. I sure didn't. So my suggestion is this. If you are not sure what you need, then learn about something — anything. Doing nothing will be a mistake. Taking the most general subjects can never hurt you. It will never take any effort to carry education around with you once you have it. The more knowledge you have, the more options you will have.

In addition to general subjects, I would like to suggest two others to study. You will need these skills to do anything in the future, from teacher to animator. One is computers. If you do not have a good working knowledge of computers and some programs, you are limiting yourself before you begin. The other skill you will need is typing. Yuck! Yes, typing. It is your link to the computer. There is no reason you should spend your life picking and pecking your way with a computer when a high school course in typing is so readily available.

Even if you choose the basic courses of mathematics, English, and science during your early years of high school, you will eventually have to start narrowing your focus. If you have a direction, these choices will be easier. But if you are like I was, you will start by eliminating the topics in which you have absolutely no interest or ability. If you are lucky, you will still be able to fill your course schedule with what remains. Either way, you will be moving forward.

My own family experience produced an interesting contrast. My brother was a year older than me and decided in about Grade 6 to be a dentist. He became a dentist and still loves it after more than twenty-five years. It took me years to find a direction, and it is still subject to change. The important thing is not to give up hope.

I know not everyone will graduate from high school. Not everyone will go on to college and university. But keep as many doors open as possible by getting an education. You can still be a waiter with a Ph.D. but you can't be a professor if you drop out of high school.

Consider your own skills and interests. Seek input from your parents and your guidance counsellor. As you do so, assess the availability of career opportunities in various fields of interest, consider the degree of difficulty and the costs associated with any educational program, and try to talk to someone actually working in a chosen field. You will need to gather many facts to make the right decisions. Ultimately, you will have to use both your head and your heart in making your decision. Just remember that only you will be living with the consequences, so make sure the choices are yours. If you have listened and gathered information, have confidence in your own decisions. In the words of Cicero, "Nobody can give you wiser advice than you can give yourself."

One difficulty faced by all young people is lack of knowledge about most careers. Television exposes them to a distorted view of some careers such as policeman, doctor, lawyer, or teacher. Most real life jobs are never portrayed at all. Careers in environmental science, child care, and many others are never shown on television. The variety of positions available in the world of business is almost unlimited.

Parents of Purples often lament that their advice is not getting through. I actually think mine did, once. When my son was going off to university, I suggested he remember one thing. He could go to 100% of the parties for one year or 80% of the parties for four years. He did the math quickly in his head and realized what was more important. He may have tried to push the 80% a little higher, but he did graduate.

This brings an opportunity to introduce the theory of rear-view mirror planning. To do it effectively involves imagining yourself as older and looking back on your life — essentially writing your future autobiography. There may be many things in the course of your life that you want to accomplish. Some, such as writing a book, can be done at any stage of life. Others, such as having children or playing football, can be done only by a specific age. Once you go past that age, there is no turning back the clock. You either do it now or never.

ATHLETICS

I believe most people see this "do it now" theory applying clearly to athletics. It is not likely you will be playing football when you are fifty. All of us know that athletes are young. A thirty-six-year-old athlete is considered a wily old veteran in the final stages of his career. So if you have any athletic dreams to be lived or abilities to be developed, you'd better do it while you can.

Purple is the time of your life when you will reach your maximum physical strength. There are many opportunities to participate in athletic activities both inside and outside of school. Use your time in Purple to experiment with as many of these athletic activities as possible. However, some of your greatest personal growth will come from choosing one or two sports in which to specialize. Then you will find out how good you can really be. What are your limits? How much discipline do you have? What is teamwork? How can you be a leader?

When it comes to making choices in life, remember this adage: The eye will see many things but the heart just a few. Pursue these. If you find an activity about which you are passionate, you will be surprised how much time you can spend at it. While you are doing what you enjoy, you will become better and better at doing it.

One other comment about opportunity: Every community has some activity or activities at which they excel. St. Catharines is a great place for rowing, Kingston is a great place for sailing, and Vancouver is a great place for skiing. Anywhere in Canada is good for hockey. Look around your own community to see what opportunities exist. If your passion is for a sport that is not easily supported locally, the cost of pursuing it goes up and the opportunity to indulge in it usually goes down, unless you make major adjustments to other parts of your life.

If an athletic activity becomes a major focus for you, make sure you live out the dream completely. You do not want to be giving yourself any speeches later in life that begin with "if only."

The physical fitness you take for granted when you are young is something you lose quickly as you age or you work hard to maintain all your life. Your physical health will have a great deal to do with how much you are able to enjoy all the other stages of your life. Good fitness habits now will be beneficial forever.

OTHER ACTIVITIES

My comments about involvement in sports are just as applicable to non-athletic activities. Many opportunities for leadership and involvement will be available in your school and your community. Take advantage of as many as you can. Remember, you learn the most when you involve yourself in activities that interest you.

Purple may be your time for adventure. Others may be keen to get on with careers and families. If adventure is calling you, my advice is to go. I had a need to travel. I do not mean I wanted to travel or I enjoyed travelling: I mean I had to travel. It was something in my soul that I needed to satisfy. It took a lot to satisfy that need. I had to live in California, hitchhike across Canada, travel from Europe to India and then overland from South Africa to Europe via the Sahara Desert.

These were very special times for me. I loved my vagabond life. In time I knew I had to move on. I remember reading why Henry David Thoreau had left his paradise on Walden Pond: "I have many more lives to lead, and I do not have any more time to spend on that one."

Would I recommend travel? Maybe. It certainly was a great education in geography and people. The more valuable lessons were about myself. It also taught me to live with very few possessions. My entire travel bag weighed less than twenty pounds. Your adventures may be in sports, politics, travel, music, or spirituality. Take the time in Purple to investigate them because the responsibilities of life will catch up with you soon.

Don't expect total support from your parents or your peers on anything that involves risk or that is considered out of the ordinary. Your parents' emotional response is to protect you from failure and disappointment. Their practical response is to get you financially self-sufficient. So you had better be prepared for two things. The first is you will have to plan to do this adventure alone. Second, you will have to figure out a way to finance it yourself. This will not be something your parents will likely want to do.

ROMANCE

If you are fortunate, you will have some intensely passionate experiences at this time in your life. Sometimes early romance is more a discovery of ourselves than of another. I would caution everyone considering early marriage to at least do a little of that rear-view mirror planning. Imagine yourself at eighty and consider this. Will it be better to have been married at age twenty, had my kids early, and then have been married for sixty years? Or would it be better to have been single and experiencing life till thirty and then be married fifty years? Let me just suggest that most of us have a great deal of personal growing to do before we can commit to another. If you do not know what your own values are, how are you going to find someone who shares them?

There are two habits you want to try to develop at this point in your life. The first is setting goals and the second is saving a percentage of your income before you spend the rest. The important thing about setting goals is to put them in writing. This has many benefits. It makes them clear. They can be reviewed to measure progress and to allow you to feel satisfaction with their accomplishment. Write your goals in a blank book and update it on a regular basis. Set goals in several areas:

- Health and fitness
- Education and career
- Financial
- Personal (family, adventure, community, travel)

Try to set these goals with a focus on both the short term (one year) and the long term (five years and more).

When it comes to saving money, you also need goals. If you have no idea what you are saving for, it is very difficult to make saving a priority. Set up a method for accumulating your savings — a separate bank account or a monthly contribution to a mutual fund. Any system that forces you to put the money in on a regular basis and then makes it inconvenient to get at will work. You must think of this money as untouchable until your desired goal is reached. If you are going to reach your personal and financial goals, budgeting and tracking your expenses on a computer program like Quicken will help.

Make saving money a habit. A habit is one of the most powerful forces on earth. Ultimately, you will become a victim of any habit, whether good or bad. If you are going to start good habits — like saving money — start now. If you are going to try to eliminate bad habits, do it now, too. It doesn't get easier to rid yourself of bad habits with age.

MONEY

Entering Purple means accepting financial responsibility, and this is one of the most critical things you need to learn at this point in your life. Many people will have no choice except to take on this responsibility because their circumstances provide no other option. Others will be fortunate to have financial assistance from their families. However, you and your parents must plan the process of gradually pushing you out of the financial nest. Too often young people are allowed to become family welfare cases and are not forced to learn money-management discipline, which will be an essential skill throughout their life. So if your parents are not pushing you from the nest, you had better be prepared to jump. Becoming financially independent may mean you do not get the red convertible today, but the skills you learn will prevent your inheritance from being squandered later in life. I am not saying that you should be financially self-supporting from your teenage years, although some of you may have to be. What I am saying is that you had better not be totally dependent.

The best situation occurs when your parents give you a clear idea of the financial resources they will provide for you. If they

Which Twin Has the Most Money?

Start saving early and let compound interest work for you!

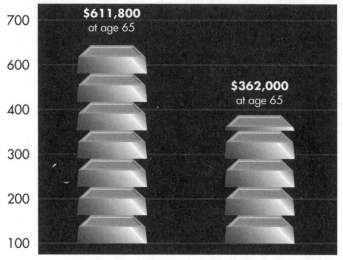

| | Sister starts saving at age 25
$2,000 x 10 yrs =
$20,000 | Brother starts saving at age 35
$2,000 x 30 yrs =
$60,000 |

Assumptions:

All money invested at the beginning of the year
10% annual rate of return
All investment income is reinvested and is in an RRSP

give you a spending allowance, what are you expected to use it for? Are they going to give you other resources and, if so, when and on what conditions?

The important thing is to understand how much money you have coming in. Then you'll know how much additional money you'll need to earn to meet your perceived consumption needs. Alternatively, you may decide to lower your needs. It is amazing how quickly this can happen when you have to accept the responsibility for earning that money. The good news is that you will be in control of your own financial life.

You do not want a situation where you have no clear idea of what your parents will provide and you continue to use the same old "tin cupping" experiences of your childhood. This occurs when you spend all your own money and then ask for and expect to receive whatever you think you need from your parents. The bad news is that you are not in control of your own financial life.

GETTING A JOB

Making your own money is a critical part of your education. Getting that first part-time or summer job is very important. It can be at McDonald's, running a paper route, or pumping gas. The important thing is that you are given responsibility for a task and are financially rewarded for its satisfactory completion. Do not underestimate how much you learn in these first jobs. You are being exposed to different styles of management and business systems. You will also learn a great deal about what you like and dislike in a job. This information will be invaluable in making your own career choices in the future. It may surprise you how you apply lessons learned on these jobs later in life.

All jobs are not boring. In fact, many jobs can revolve around other interests you have developed. For example, if you have spent your time becoming a competitive figure skater, you may get a job teaching figure skating. Or, if your goal is to work with kids and you love to canoe, perhaps a job at a summer camp can satisfy both interests. If you have the opportunity and freedom to choose between a position providing great experience and one that provides good money, go for the experience. You will have a chance to get the money later, provided you have acquired the necessary skills.

This is all well and good if you can find a job. How do you do that? Unfortunately, getting a job involves selling. You have to

sell yourself to an employer. This is always easier if you are recommended by a friend. That way you are more likely to know
something about the business and its needs, but in the end, you
will have to meet these potential employers. Do not sit back and
hope they find you. Do not just send out résumés. Meet potential employers face to face. If you want a job, you will have to
ask for it and sell yourself. Just remember, selling is not order
taking. Not everyone will say yes. However, you only need one
yes, so it doesn't matter how many times you get a no before
you get a yes. This selling of yourself continues throughout your
life, so you may as well get used to it and get good at doing it.

Two of the best learning experiences for young people are in
starting their own business and working in a family business. In
both situations you will be exposed firsthand to all aspects of
a business. They also provide a perfect opportunity to find out
your level of interest and talent. In the long term, this could save
a lot of turmoil for everyone concerned. Do not underestimate
what you are learning. The principles of a business are the same
whether it be large or small.

Creating a business of your own is like earning a Master's
degree in life. These business opportunities are endless — house
painting, lawn mowing and landscaping services, or a computer-
based business such as Web page design. Whatever the business,
the experience will be one of unbelievable personal growth. You
will first have to envision the business or service, research the
business, then plan to create it, including the financial and human
resources required. You will have to sell the service, deliver a
quality product, determine budgets and costs in order to effectively bill and collect for the service, manage personnel and
customer relations, and manage your own time. If you can do all
that and make a profit, you will deserve the informal Master's
degree.

DEBT

Managing money can be a real problem. You can't escape this fact just because you are young. Statistics indicate that the average university student graduates with debts around $25,000. That is a ball and chain that will have to be dealt with before you can move on to all the other plans you have for your life.

Debt is not fun, but sometimes it is necessary. Sometimes it can even be profitable if the money is being used in a way that generates more income. But whether you are young or old, in business or not, being free of debt is always best. Banks and other lending institutions can be very helpful. However, you must remember that their purpose is to make a profit for the bank. They are not altruistic. Above all, you must realize that they want the money paid back. This is not a gift. They will also charge you interest in the meantime.

As a general rule, try not to borrow money unless it is for an asset that will at least hold its value, such as a house. You may need to borrow for a business, hoping that the business profits will pay off the loan. When you borrow for a business, the interest can be deducted from your income as an expense for income tax purposes.

Borrowing money to enhance your lifestyle is very tempting. Remember, you always have to pay the amount back out of future income, and the interest is an additional expense. So, when the day of reckoning comes, and it will come, you will have to lower your lifestyle again, not an easy thing to do.

Students should make every effort to graduate debt free. It will leave you unencumbered to seek your adventures. It leaves you ready to move on to the next steps in life, and in the meantime, you will have developed terrific money-management skills.

Education costs are often prohibitive, but there are some ways to lessen the burden. Seek out every source that can help you pay these costs. Look for grants, loans, and bursaries. The federal government has introduced the Canada Millennium Scholarships Foundation to start in the year 2000. For full-time students, the scholarships will average $3,000 a year, to a total of $15,000 over four academic years of study towards undergraduate degrees, diplomas, or certificates.

Here are some more suggestions to keep costs down:

- Attend a university or college close to home.
- If you go away to school, live close enough that you can walk so you do not need to pay for transportation or parking.
- Do not own a car if you can prevent it. Get a bike instead.
- If you can get a part-time job for Friday and Saturday night at a pub or restaurant where there are lots of other young people, you can earn money instead of spending it and you will still be part of the action.
- Certain part-time jobs allow you freedom to do some studying while on the job (e.g., night manager of a car rental agency).
- Do not have a credit card — the temptation to use it is too great.
- Set up a realistic budget so you have some idea of the income you will need.
- Buy used textbooks and computer equipment whenever possible.
- Do not smoke.
- Be conscious of the big luxuries (ski trips, restaurants, movies) and the little luxuries (coffee, beer). They do add up.

- Do not try to keep up with the Joneses who live it up on student loans or someone else's money. They will pay later, trust me.
- Make a bit of a game out of getting by on very little. It may just surprise you how many activities are free.

If there are special events in your plans, budget for them. This way you not only get to do them but you get to do them right. After all, if you are going to go to Paris, you had better be able to afford to go up the Eiffel Tower when you get there.

LOOKING BACK

Bertrand Russell was of the opinion that society will forgive anything you do before thirty, so relax. Don't take yourself too seriously. Nothing you choose to do now is necessarily final. As a matter of fact, it almost certainly will change many times.

I have a message to all those competitive types out there: This is not a race. Getting to the next stage sooner is not a victory. If you leave any stage before you have accomplished the things you wanted, it is a mistake. You may get a chance to correct this later, but don't count on it.

Hopefully, you have maximized your experiences, minimized your debts, and started some good habits. Through education and adventure you have developed your self-confidence. You are secure in your own masculinity or femininity.

Remember from White how you will know when you are ready to move on from Purple? That's right, check out your parents to see if they are getting any smarter. In addition, you will find within yourself a willingness and a desire to seek your own answers to what I call life's three big questions, which I will ask you in Green.

These questions may sound serious, they may even be intimidating, but you can't go through life living out of a knapsack with all your junk stored at your parents' forever.

So, hang on because it's time to move on to Green.

GREEN
ESTABLISHING ROOTS

—

Green involves trying to answer the three big questions: Where do you want to live? What do you want to do? And who do you want to be with?

When you think of Where, What, and Who, you ask yourself which comes first. This is similar to what came first, the chicken or the egg? I know this sounds a little like the Abbott and Costello skit, "Who's on first?" However, these issues are all of great importance to your growth and happiness. A decision on one issue will affect the others. For example, if you want to be a ski instructor in Whistler, you may not be able to marry a wheat farmer from Regina without making major sacrifices. If you want a career in nuclear physics, you may not be able to live in Picton, Ontario.

When making a Who, Where, or What decision, keep their interdependence in mind. Life will not let you procrastinate too long before it will force you to make choices. The clearer your vision of the future, the more you know what you want, the easier it is to make these choices.

The timing of these decisions is not always predictable.

However, it's the easiest if you answer What first, then Where, and finally Who. In doing it in this order, you are giving your Who all the information before he or she chooses too. Hopefully, he or she who has made his or her own What and Where decisions, so you have equal information. Nevertheless, the circumstances of your life may dictate a different order. As always, play the cards you're dealt.

I'm going to talk about each decision and some of the thoughts you should consider in making your choices.

WHERE

This is likely the topic most people just let happen, to their detriment. They make decisions based on where they are now, where someone else tells them to go, or where someone else is located. Too little thought is given to the limitations these decisions have on other factors in their life and the impact it may have on their happiness.

When you enter the Green stage of your life and begin to ponder where you want to be, some of the issues you should consider are:

- How close do I want to be to family and friends?
- Where are career opportunities the best for me?
- In what size of community will I be most comfortable?
- Will this community meet the needs of my significant other?
- Will this community support my other lifestyle needs such as religion, recreation, language, and sexual orientation?
- How far am I prepared to commute?
- What impact will the cost of living have on my lifestyle?

These questions can't be answered for you by anyone else. Your siblings will come to completely different conclusions than you. Just keep Shakespeare's words in mind: "To thine own self be true."

Decisions about Where get more complicated when you add a Who and, if you're ambitious, a What. Relax, no Where decision is final. In fact, most people in North America move several times during a lifetime.

WHO

Finding a Who is easy, all you have to do is find someone else just as much in need of a relationship as you are and, abracadabra, you are in love. Now, finding someone with whom you share common values and with whom you can develop a level of intimacy sustainable over a lifetime is not as easy as simply falling in love.

Before you can find Who you had better find You. This requires developing your personal identity and maturity to the point that Who will choose You when the opportunity presents itself. I have chosen to put this issue in Green because, statistically, this is when most people make this decision. You may have to make more than one Who decision in your lifetime. Don't be in a rush. The Who part of your life can be delayed. Females face a little more time pressure than males because of the biological clock, but it shouldn't become an issue until well into Red.

Choosing your Who has little to do with starting the race fast. It's all about still being there at the finish line. There is an enormous level of satisfaction in looking back over a lifetime of shared experiences, which can never be attained if your partners constantly change.

Some questions you can ask yourself before making your Who choice are:

- Am I mature enough to support another person's needs?
- Is the attraction more than physical?
- Can I accept his or her spending habits?
- Can I accept his or her lifestyle habits, such as smoking and drinking?
- Can I accept his or her religious beliefs?
- Do we have a similar sense of humour?
- Are our levels of ambition compatible?
- Are our goals for a family compatible?
- Are our geographic location needs compatible?
- Do we share lifestyle interests?
- How does he or she treat the other important people in his or her life, such as parents, friends, co-workers, and children?
- Does he or she always treat me with respect?
- What are the things I would want him or her to change? Is he or she capable of changing any of them? Am I sure?

These are a lot of factors to consider. And, knowing how much change will occur in our fast-paced lives, it is almost miraculous when two people do accommodate their different growth patterns and still develop a level of intimacy. I think of George Bernard Shaw's summary of the emotions and risks involved in choosing a mate: "When two people are under the influence of the most violent, most insane, most delusive, and most transient of passions, they are required to swear that they will remain in that excited, abnormal, and exhausting condition continuously until death do them part." Those words should scare some of you back to reality! Ultimately, this is your most important decision. It is also the decision most fraught with emotional and financial troubles if you have to make a change.

WHAT

Choosing your What is much easier than Where or Who. Still, you should expect to fail several times before you find your success. I use the word fail here deliberately. Failure is not necessarily bad, it's just the result of experimentation. Failing is how we learn.

The What of your life will be very important in helping you establish your personal identity. Your What establishes your financial status, helps provide focus and meaning to your life, and also provides one of the greatest opportunities to give leadership and mentoring to other people. A great deal of your personal satisfaction will come from What you choose to do in your career.

Some people at this point in life will attempt to make permanent commitments so everything will be set for the rest of their lives. After some time they may find that they feel trapped.

Others will follow a course of non-commitment and transience. At the other extreme are those who rush into being caregivers. None of these options is wrong or right. The truth is that most people just do not know where their ideal future lies at this stage of life. Many people simply fall into what is available and try to make the best of it. The downside of this strategy is they never really do an assessment of their choices. They simply drift. But Green is a time of great opportunity to explore your own goals.

The place to start in self-assessment is usually by identifying and eliminating what you do *not* want to do. Make sure you are eliminating things based on your own knowledge and not prejudice or emotional reaction. I never imagined I would make a career in sales. Only 5% of university graduates ever think they will end up in sales, but a substantially higher number end up in some type of sales position. I turned out to be one of them.

This is the secret, to eventually find something you like to do, something you find absorbing. When people are asked What they are looking for, they usually reply, "All I want is a really good job." Unfortunately, life doesn't work that way. It won't come to you. You will have to make things happen: "Find something you like doing, and keep doing it for a long period of time."

How do you find something you like doing? Most people experiment. Here are some ideas to reduce frustrating trial and error.

- Start by listing all the things you have been good at and enjoyed doing up till now. Don't be bashful.
- List all your skills and talents, including the physical, intellectual, emotional, social, and spiritual.
- Be clear about what you don't want to do.
- List all the people you admire and why.
- Using rear-view mirror planning, make a list of all the things you would like to have accomplished and done in your life by the time you're ninety.
- Make a list of occupations that could allow you to accomplish some of these items.
- Focus on areas in which you have some advantage. This could be a specific skill, experience, or education. It could be a personal contact. This probably narrows the list down and leaves only ideas that excite you. If there is only one idea left, your answer is obvious.

Identify three people you know or can be introduced to who are involved in this field and ask for their help. Explain your interest and ask them, "If you were in my shoes, what would you do?" Listen closely to the answer, noting the names of anybody they say they would talk to. Call these people and mention who gave you their name, and ask for their help. Some of these leads will turn out to be dead ends. Ultimately, one will pay off. However, you will learn something from every interview.

You will be surprised how people who may not have a job for you will be willing to help you. As you gain knowledge about your chosen field, you may find yourself getting even more enthusiastic about this career path, or you may find your interest decreases. Either way, the exercise will be helpful. If you find you want to choose a different field, start the process over with three different people.

In Purple we discussed how getting a job requires you to be in sales. You can't sit back and wait for the order to come. Once you are involved in a field of real interest to you, your performance will create opportunities. Your expanded contacts make it easier to find out what other possibilities exist. Getting started is the toughest step. Just remember, if it was easy, everyone would do it. They don't. So you will stand out. One last piece of advice; don't give up. This is a sales job in which you only have to make one sale. You never know if it will be on the next call.

Once you have a position it can bring you happiness and contentment. There is one other offshoot: Doing something you like for a long period of time is the only real hope of obtaining wealth. The enjoyment is guaranteed, but the wealth is only a maybe. Let's talk for a little about why this is the case.

Finding something you like allows you to persist without knowing it. You just keep doing more and learning more than other people. Ultimately, you become very good at it, just as we discussed in Purple regarding an athletic activity. In addition, if you are doing something you like, it is much easier to be patient. Success does not often come quickly. Normally, it will require a period of ten to twenty years, sometimes longer. If you are not absorbed by what you are doing, you simply will not wait.

This does not mean you can never make changes. In fact, you

will almost certainly *have* to make them. Often these are just career adjustments that allow you to concentrate more on the things you like. Frequently, the competence of your work will attract the attention of others and they will make a financially attractive offer to use or retain you and your skills. Or you may be compelled to establish your own business to do things the way you think they should be done.

One of the biggest reasons people resist change is the need for the affirmation of others. They want other people to think that what they are doing is okay. Nobody else can ever decide for you. What absorbs you will not likely absorb anyone else. You will always make a mistake if you ask yourself, "What will other people think?" Ultimately, other people will support you if they perceive you are happy with your own decisions. They will also sympathize with you if they perceive you are not happy. They will simply mirror your own feelings.

How do you know when you have found your What? The first test you can give yourself to find out how much you enjoy what you are doing is to ask yourself how many of the petty details of your job irritate you. People who are absorbed by their job hardly notice these details. The other test you can perform on yourself is the time test. Does time seem to pass quickly when you are doing your job? Does the day seem to be over almost before you start? Or are you a clock watcher, and the two hours to coffee break seem like an eternity?

If the petty stuff irritates you or if time passes slowly, you are not likely absorbed by what you are doing. You will have to make changes. These changes do not necessarily have to be large. However, the more your irritation, the bigger the change will likely have to be. When making changes, be sure you know where the problem lies. Do not change your job if your problem is in a relationship, for instance.

You might be asking yourself why nobody ever seems to talk about how much they love their jobs. This is a built-in defence mechanism. They are scared to tell people how absorbing they find their job in case someone takes it away from them. They are even less willing to admit that, for them, the job is actually easy. So don't listen to what people say about their job; instead, watch what they are doing. You can quickly spot those who are absorbed. You can see it in their attitude and their productivity. But mostly you will see it in the high quality and originality of their work.

This originality is how you obtain wealth. What the market is ultimately willing to pay a premium for is something that is original, something that is authentic, whether it is a product or a service. People will pay handsomely to obtain this authenticity. You can't do something original unless you are absorbed by your work. In every field it takes years of involvement just to get to the frontier, and a true passion to go beyond it into something original. To be original, you will need to continually narrow your field of specialty until you find something you do very well.

Some people will be passionate about a hobby or an avocation that is not financially rewarding, so they may choose a job that pays the bills and frees them up to do more of what they love in their spare time. Stay alert for a surprise. If you become the best at something, you never know when opportunity will come looking for you.

There is a memorable scene in the movie *City Slickers* that captures the need to focus, the scene between Billy Crystal, who plays a middle-aged businessman on vacation at a dude ranch, and Jack Palance, who plays a snarly old cowhand. Here's how the conversation goes.

Palance: "How old are you? Thirty-eight?"

Crystal: "Thirty-nine."

Palance: "Yeah. You all come out here about the same age. Same problems. Spend fifty weeks a year getting knots in your rope — then you think two weeks up here will untie them for you. None of you get it. (Long pause) Do you know what the secret of life is?"

Crystal: "No, what?"

Palance: "It's this." (Holds up his index finger)

Crystal: "Your finger?"

Palance: "One thing. Just one thing. You stick to that and everything else don't mean nothing."

Crystal: "That's great, but what's the one thing?"

Palance: "That's what you've got to figure out."

Since we are talking about the movies, let me share a story of a public school friend of mine. He was always bright but never very committed to school. He was much more involved in other activities. He was a trendsetter in his clothing. He also danced to the beat of his own drum when it came to activities. He was involved in go-kart racing, model airplanes, and photography. After scraping through high school with a record of discipline problems, he went to Ryerson Institute of Technology in Toronto to study photography. He was expelled. Then he joined two other guys in a business venture in which they created a movie camera that can be suspended from a helicopter. They had to go to England to try to get the business started, but the partners eventually left because they were not making any money. My friend moved to California and kept at it for over twenty years. I had lost track of him until it was announced that he had won an Oscar for his aerial photography. The next movie I went to see was *Twister*, and there in the credits, the screen was filled with the name of Ron Goodman.

GROWING

Green is a time for growth. This is when you plant the seed for a life's work. The choices you make here will set a trend for your life. The ultimate satisfaction in life is described by columnist Whit Hobbs: "Success is waking up in the morning, whoever you are, wherever you are, however old or young, and bounding out of bed because there's something out there that you love to do, that you believe in, that you are good at. Something that's bigger than you are, and you can hardly wait to get at it again."

Before we start on all the financial stuff you might be asking, What happened to all the adventure? Does it get sacrificed to the Who, Where, and What? No, it doesn't. Green is about growing. All of the same rear-view mirror theories discussed in Purple still apply. There are adventures you will want to continue pursuing. Going to Australia in Green, for example, is a different experience than going when you are in Gold. If your fantasy is to take up scuba diving, become an actor, or learn a language, now is the time to do it. Life is in the living.

Unfortunately, life does not let us do all the things we want to do. If you decide to take a job, it may mean you do not get to ski in Whistler for the winter, for instance. And if you do go to Whistler, you may be going further into debt. Trade-offs are a fact of life. Everybody else has to make them, and so will you. When making these decisions it is easier from that rear-view mirror perspective by asking yourself, "When I am ninety, what will I have been more proud to have done?"

One final instruction: Relax. Minds can be changed and mistakes can be corrected. However, time cannot be recaptured.

MONEY

Green brings with it financial opportunities and responsibilities. But before you get started on the opportunities of Green, let's just review how you left Purple. We recommended a course of action that would allow you to leave Purple with a good education, a variety of adventures and experiences, and no debt.

How did you do with that no debt item? If you didn't quite get there, then guess what becomes a major priority in Green? To make choices, you need freedom. Debt takes away your freedom. The more debt, the less freedom, until there is none at all.

So how do you reduce debt? Simple: Spend less than you earn and apply the difference to the debt. This is simple to say, but not to do. However, one of my great mentors taught me this basic method for understanding personal financial matters: "If your outgo exceeds your income, your upkeep becomes your downfall."

The financial matters you need to address in Green include more than managing expenses and debt. They include saving, pension planning, protecting income and financial status, as well as planning for a home. These are all worthwhile goals, so you would assume everyone would accomplish them. Not so.

Why not? Who are the enemies of these outcomes? Is it the temptations from the car dealers, the travel agents, the retailers? No, it's you. So let's take a look at some ways you can manage your expenses a little more effectively.

- Pay with cash. Don't use credit cards. Have only one credit card — one with no fees — available for convenience. Pay it off in full every month. Don't pay the exorbitant interest rates associated with these cards — and don't use them for impulse purchases.

- Loan consolidation is a fool's game if you do not apply the "savings" in interest to the principal every month. Just because someone agrees to lend you more money doesn't mean you should take it. This is money they will want paid back with interest. So if you reduce your payments but continue to spend, all you have done is dig the hole a little deeper.

- Automobiles are a marvellous invention. They are often essential, and they are always expensive. The average cost to run and maintain a car is about $7,000 per year. So if you can walk to work and eliminate the need to own a vehicle, and just rent when necessary, you are ahead of the game. If a vehicle is a necessity, pay cash for it. Leasing is a different word for debt, and you will end up with car payments forever. Only buy what you need. After a couple of weeks, the glory of a fancy new car is gone and it becomes just a mode of transportation. Find a mechanic you trust and take your car in to the shop for regular maintenance. Plan to keep the car for a long time because depreciation and sales taxes are killers.

- Prepare a list before you go to the grocery store. Only buy what is on the list. Always do comparisons. Buy non-perishables in bulk. Buy things that are in season. Avoid convenience foods. I have included a copy of my grocery guide. Each classification is listed in the order I come to it in the store. It sure is quick to shop that way.

- Don't smoke. This may only save $3 per day, but that adds up to $1,000 a year.

- Don't buy lottery tickets. Our taxes are high enough without volunteering to pay more. Remember, the house always wins.

- Could you live in less expensive accommodation? Could

Grocery List

| FRUIT | | BAKING | OTHER FOOD |

| VEGETABLES | | OTHER DRY |

| DAIRY | | CLEANING | PAPER |

| MEAT | BREAD | KITCHEN | BATHROOM |

| CANS | CEREAL | FROZEN |

you live in the same place and have a roommate to share costs? Could you pay the same and live within walking distance of work, thus eliminating transportation costs and saving time?

- Before buying new clothes, take a look in your closet to make sure you need them. You may be throwing things out before they wear out. Buy clothing in styles that don't go out of fashion. Buy things you need when they're on sale. Don't be too snobbish to check out the consignment shops.

- The library can provide unlimited free entertainment. You can get most magazines, books, and newspapers there for free.

- Wait until a movie comes out on video or television. If you must see it at the theatre, go to the matinee.

- Take vacations closer to home to reduce transportation costs. If you must fly, book well in advance and search out special fares. Costs can vary widely.

- Reduce the number of times you go to restaurants or order out for food. Invite friends to come for a barbecue to which the guests bring their own food. If you go to a restaurant, reduce or eliminate alcohol, share one dessert, and skip the coffee.

- Monitor the cost of your hobbies to ensure that they are not getting out of control. Trust me, the latest in golf or ski equipment will not make you that much more skilled. Most of the difference is hype and marketing.

- Assess your fitness programs. It does not cost a lot to jog and do pushups. A personal trainer and a private club are luxuries.

- Weddings last one day. Make sure you are not paying for one for several years. If your parents want to pay for everything, it's their problem. Otherwise, set a budget and don't get carried away with the emotion of making the perfect day. Remember, people come because of who you are and not because of the size of the bouquets. Regard the part about the ring being worth two months' salary as jeweller's hype. Honeymoons are really about time together, not where you go, so stay within your financial limits.

- Keep a record of your expenses. We talked about this in Purple, but it applies now, and in the future, just as much. Computer programs are available to help you.

- Prepare your own income tax returns. This can be done on an inexpensive computer program or manually. Knowledge is power. Knowing how significantly taxes affect our lives makes your return something you cannot completely delegate to someone else. You must understand planning opportunities yourself. If your tax returns get complicated, use a professional but stay involved. Don't abandon the responsibility. Nobody else will ever care as much about your situation as you do.

SAVING

Saving money — what a thought. Maybe we are finally ready to start building a positive net worth rather than just getting out of debt.

There are two methods of saving money. One is to establish a set budget for expenses and save the rest. The other is to take the savings out first and spend the rest. Just make sure you don't spend more than the rest. Unfortunately, I have come to know that devil called human nature, so my belief is that you must always take the savings out first — budget or no budget.

Fortunately, there are many easy ways to siphon off the savings portion of your income. You can set up a program at work to have money deducted for Canada Savings Bonds. All mutual funds can be purchased on an automatic monthly withdrawal. Your bank will transfer a set amount each month from your chequing account into a savings account. Establishing a mortgage payment above the minimum is another form of saving, as you are increasing the amount of money going to pay down the outstanding principal. Just remember, you are much less likely to spend what you do not see.

Saving money is always easier if you have a goal in mind as to what the money will be used for — perhaps a wedding, a down payment on a home, capital to start a business, or a car. The clearer the goal, the less likely you are to touch the money in the meantime.

Saving money, pension planning, or investing can be complicated topics, but ultimately they come down to five key points. Each is important, but you do not even need to think about Priority 4 if you did not do Priority 1.

Priority 1 — Set money aside regularly.

Priority 2 — Don't touch it until your goal is reached.

Priority 3 — Make sure the capital is safe.

Priority 4 — Get the best rate of return you can.

Priority 5 — Be aware of the effect of income taxes on your rate of return.

When you are thinking about saving or investing, never put the cart ahead of the horse. Frankly, you do not want them running side by side either. Focus on the priorities one at a time and in order.

The best story about the return on your money not being that important came from a legendary financial adviser and speaker, the late John Savage. John called it his tin can theory.

If you had money to save each month and you put equal amounts in a tin can and in a savings account with 5% interest, in ten years where do you think you would have the most money?

Before you answer, remember that with the savings account you get interest on your money but you can also get your hands on the money any time you want. With the tin can, you do not get interest on your money but this tin can is unique because it opens only long enough for you to put the money in, then it is slammed shut and you cannot get at the money for ten years.

After that period of time, where do you think you would have the most money?

Would the answer be any different if the interest rate were 12%? Most people acknowledge that they would have more money in the tin can no matter the interest rate. We all realize that somewhere during that ten years, given a chance, we would have spent some or all of the money in the bank account. The rate of return is secondary. Before getting excited about a tax-effective rate of return, remember that setting aside the money, not touching it, and protecting your capital come first.

RRSPs

The best savings vehicle is a Registered Retirement Savings Plan (RRSP), which is perfectly designed to support my five priorities. First, the government creates a tax advantage and a sense of urgency to put in the money. Then they make it a tax disadvantage to take the money out before retirement. The returns in an RRSP are enhanced through tax deferral. The deduction of the contribution on your income tax return and the deferral of the tax on the growth are an unbeatable combination.

We will spend more time on RRSPs in Red and Gold. Let's just say that you should have one. Starting early is a terrific advantage. Set up a monthly withdrawal plan as soon as you are able.

Here's a case study that points out the merits of starting your RRSP early. A woman, age twenty-five, invests $2,000 a year in an RRSP at the beginning of each year for ten years, then stops. She doesn't put another cent into that RRSP. It grows at a 10% average annual compounding rate of return. Her twin brother doesn't think about investing for retirement until he's thirty-five. Then he invests $2,000 in an RRSP at the beginning of each year, but he does it for thirty years. He gets a 10% rate of return, too.

Guess who is ahead when they're both sixty-five? The woman. Her $20,000 capital outlay will have grown to over $611,000. Her brother's $60,000 investment will have grown to about $362,000.

Both examples show the magic of compounding. Remember that Rule of 72 we talked about way back in White? Divide the interest rate into 72 to find out how many years it takes for money to double. The message is clear. Start early, think long term, and you have a better chance of winding up ahead.

Some people may be fortunate enough to have a pension plan at their place of employment. Take full advantage of it but still contribute to your own RRSP. Maximizing your RRSP contribution is your best bet for a retirement that's free of financial worry. We will repeat this mantra at all stages.

Setting up an RRSP or any financial plan can be done at most major financial institutions. However, finding a professional financial adviser you can relate to and work with over the years is the most reliable method of overcoming your own inertia, procrastination, and lack of knowledge. His or her advice will prove very helpful in building your financial future. Choose a planner who is more interested in educating you than impressing you. All the decisions will still have to be yours — the planner is only the facilitator. Most financial advisers are paid a commission by the financial institution, so there is no direct cost to you. The rate of commission varies with different products. Your advisor should clearly explain the selection of products to you.

INSURANCE

Two other topics that a financial adviser should be able to help you with are life insurance and disability insurance. These are not exciting topics, but they are essential to a proper financial plan.

You require enough life insurance to eliminate your debts on your death. Now is no time to leave them to your parents or your new spouse. If you are married or in a significant relationship, you should be planning to provide enough capital so that your partner's lifestyle is not significantly altered by your death. There are two main types of life insurance: term insurance and permanent insurance. Stated simply, term insurance is initially less expensive and pays only if you die within a preset period of time — the term. Permanent insurance pays when you die and is in force throughout your lifetime as long as you continue to pay the premiums. Many arguments persist as to which type of coverage you should have. For most people some combination of permanent and term makes the most sense. Your financial planner can explain the differences in cost and coverage.

Disability is statistically more likely to happen to you during your working years than death. It can create devastating personal and financial consequences but it is significantly easier to deal with the personal side if the financial challenges can be dealt with by a disability insurance program. Everyone has some basic protection through the Canada Pension Plan. In addition, you should always take advantage of any long-term disability coverage your employer offers in an employee benefit package. This is also true for life insurance and enhanced medical coverage. Provide your financial adviser with your employee benefits book to make sure that your coverage is adequate. Group disability insurance obtained through your employer is significantly less expensive than a personal policy. However, a personal contract is something you can own for your working life and it is not at risk if you change employment. Have your adviser point out these differences to you. Be sure you are covered by long-term disability insurance and don't pinch pennies.

LOOKING AHEAD

What's that sound you hear? Is it the sound of a promotion, or the sound of you starting your own business or buying your own home, or the sound of a baby crying as you start your own family? It's the sound of Red approaching.

Hopefully, you are leaving Green doing What you like doing. You are happy Where you are living and Who you are with. You have gotten rid of your debts, saved some money, started your RRSP, and insured yourself; all of this while you experienced life to its fullest. If you have done all this, you personify what Green is all about.

You have grown.

RED

AMBITION AND ACCOMPLISHMENT

—

It's show time. All that education, all that experience you have gained, prepares you to be successful and happy with your life. That life takes place in Red.

Red is about marriage and family. It may also be about divorce. Red is when most people have to deal with the care and eventual death of parents. At the same time, they are parents themselves. Red is when you begin to understand that it takes effort to maintain your health and weight. Red is when you can no longer live with other people's image of success. You have to define it for yourself.

Red is about managing risk, in your career and with your money. You will have to learn a lot about yourself to make the right choices. Take on too much risk and you live a life of stress, a life out of balance. If you take on too little, you will wake up some day and realize life just passed you by.

Red is about saving and investing. Red is when you pay more in taxes than you get back in services. Taxes are something you need to know about. Red is about providing insurance for your family's financial security.

Red is the culmination of what you prepared for in White, Purple, and Green. It is also the place where you put in the foundation so you can fulfill your goals for Gold, Silver, and Grey. Red is the period of life when differences between men and women become most visible. However, the increasing independence of women is blurring the lines.

MEN AND WOMEN

Men at this stage have traditionally made career the central focus of their lives. All of the rewards and recognition provided by our society support this career focus. Women are in transition. In the past, being a mother and a wife won the praise and support of society. Today, a woman has more choices, choices that aren't going to be fully supported no matter which ones she makes. Should she make career the focus and maintain full independence? Should she temporarily sacrifice career for family? There are no right answers. It is clear that women have more pressures on them. On the career front, their pressures are similar to men's. On the home front, they may be getting more help from spouses than in the past but their own expectations of their role produces an additional burden of guilt.

The working women of today are pioneering a future of balance between career and family. Being a pioneer involves struggle as well as learning by trial and error. It means accepting that you can't achieve fulfillment through someone else. You have to define fulfillment alone and you have to attain it alone. This does not mean you have to *be* alone. Your ability to give to others, whether as a mother, partner, or colleague, is enhanced by your growing self-confidence. These skills will prepare women to take more and more leadership roles in the future.

HEALTH

Increasingly, people seek balance in their lives between personal health, family intimacy, and career satisfaction. Balance can be elusive. It does not mean equal time for each part. If you have a health or business problem, you will have to focus on this area almost exclusively for a period of time to get it back under control. Sometimes you have to get out of balance in order to grow. Only then can you find equilibrium at a higher level.

Your health is critical to satisfaction at all stages of life. Until now, nature has been quite forgiving of your poor diet, lack of exercise, irregular sleeping habits, and alcohol and tobacco use. They have taken their toll, but only now do the effects become visible. Unless you have some unexplainable need to get to Grey and beyond quickly, you had better start disciplining yourself now. The list of things you need to do is not long, but the tasks aren't easy.

- The closest thing to an anti-aging pill is regular exercise. It increases strength, keeps blood pressure down, and increases bone mass. As you age, you begin to lose strength, your blood pressure may increase, and your bone mass lessen. Your exercise program should include strength, flexibility, and aerobic aspects. As Nike says, "Just do it."
- Don't smoke.
- Eat a balanced diet. Some selective use of supplements may be helpful, but talk to your doctor before embracing the latest fad diet.
- Use alcohol moderately, or not at all.
- Get enough sleep, usually seven to eight hours a night.
- Have a physical examination regularly.

A healthy lifestyle can add years to your life and life to your years. Start now and make it part of your life.

PRIORITIES

Another aspect of balance at this stage involves learning and participating in activities that you will be able to enjoy after your active working career is over. Do not wait until you are retired to start them. A small sample of these activities includes hiking, golf, community volunteering, reading, using the Internet, gardening, and travel. What provides balance and perspective to your life today may become a central focus later.

Many people cite their family as their major priority. Concentrating on your family involves commitment to others, with the focus on marriage and parenting. On the other hand, you may be confronted with the upheaval of divorce.

MARRIAGE

I asked Dennis Boyd, a registered psychologist, for some suggestions on how to develop and maintain a successful marriage. He had the following suggestions. I believe they are a good guide for any relationship. Staying married may have more impact on your financial planning than anything else you do.

- Have an attitude of openness to growth. Everyone has to grow. Everyone changes, you as well as your partner. If one or both are not flexible, power struggles become the rule.
- Make peace with your past. We are a product of our history. The old saying that those who ignore history are destined to repeat it is certainly true of relationships. An examination of other relationships we have been part of, or affected by, can provide valuable lessons.

- Love unconditionally. This means commitment, loving even in negative situations.
- Become a better listener. Create regular opportunities to talk to each other. Pay attention to more than the words. Listen to the meaning or the underlying needs that are being expressed.
- Be flexible and be prepared to compromise. A high value must be placed on joint decision making. A marriage is a joining of two selves, and for it to survive, neither individual can be superior.
- Forgive frequently. Accept the fact that you may be part of the problem.
- Have fun or play. Just because you are married doesn't mean you can't plan a date together. Watch less television. Do something together that will encourage interaction.
- Encourage always. This is a good rule for working with people at any time, so a marriage should not be an exception.

Parenting adds complexity to a marriage. In addition to the above guidelines for marriage, add these:

- Parenting is a team effort. Collaborate your efforts and support the efforts of each other.
- Tell and show the children you love them. You can't do this too much.
- Give your children your most valuable resource, your time. In return, you get their time. They may teach you more than you realize.
- Walk the talk. Remember what we said in White, "Your actions speak so loudly, they can't hear what you're saying."

Marriage and family play an integral role in many people's lives. When things do not go well here, it makes for considerable upheaval everywhere else. Unfortunately, over a third of all marriages do not work out. In addition to huge emotional costs, nothing is more disruptive to a family's financial plan than divorce. However, when divorce does happen, the following suggestions may help minimize the emotional and financial cost to everyone involved.

- The child always comes first.
- The child has a right to two parents, except in clear cases of abuse. Today you share parenting, tomorrow you will share grandparenting. Try to create a harmonious situation for the child. Who cares if you have to eat a little crow or bite your tongue a lot? Your children are worth it. This harmony requires compromise, flexibility, and acknowledgment by all parties.
- Interaction can be minimized and centred on the child. Keep the disagreements between the two of you. Discuss them away from the children. Do not force the kids to pick sides. Keep the disagreements nonviolent. Seek professional help so you can focus on the essential things needed for the child. Set clear boundaries and establish areas of common ground between the two of you.
- Divorce is not abnormal. People who get divorced are not bad people. People who are divorced are not failures.
- Children of divorced parents can be just as well adjusted as anyone else. They will benefit when divorced parents are growing and happy. Children can gain through expanded family relationships created by remarriage, such as stepparents, step-siblings, half-siblings, and step-grandparents.

- Anger takes its toll on you and prevents your moving forward with your life. Remember, your former spouse is still the parent of your child. He or she couldn't be all bad. After all, you did marry him or her.
- When it comes to dividing financial assets, try to stay out of the adversarial environment that is usually created in the courts. Working with a professional mediator seems to be a more constructive place to start. Family law is clear about division of assets. Trying to fight the law impoverishes both of you to the betterment of the lawyers. You'll end up where the law said you would anyway.
- Maintaining a civil relationship with a former spouse allows an integration of your past history and helps to create a sense of wholeness to your life. You can never deny what has been shared.
- Marriage is not a bad thing or to be feared. Over 80% of all divorced people end up remarried.

Red is an emotional time. This is the sandwich time of life. In addition to all your own concerns about career and marriage, you are a parent with responsibilities to your children, but this is also the time that your parents can even the score by depending on you more and more. No one said being an adult was easy, but life goes on. You still have a career to consider and a financial plan to meet.

MONEY

ATTITUDES ABOUT MONEY
Before we even start talking about your career, we have to address the most basic of issues, your financial values and your

attitude towards money. If these are clarified, it makes all other planning much easier. We will also take a quick look at what the rich are really like and not what television says they are like.

Some very good books deal with people's attitudes to money matters. Two I recommend are *Your Money Personality*, by Dr. Kathleen Gurney, and *Your Money or Your Life*, by Joe Dominguez and Vicki Robin.

Dr. Gurney describes nine styles of handling money, each one with a different set of habits and values. I have reduced the list to just three types of money handlers: spenders, savers, and entrepreneurs.

SPENDERS

Spenders are by far the most common among us. After all, we have a huge advertising industry totally focused on getting us to participate. I know you can't live without spending. The big problem comes when you spend before you save. If by some fluke you accidentally end up with extra cash, do you put it in a no-touch pile? No, of course not. You are a spender.

What's wrong with being a spender? After all, "you only live once," and "you can't take it with you." Besides the obvious — it leads to poor financial planning — there are three key reasons not to be a spender.

1. Debt removes freedom. You can be imprisoned in your own cash-flow needs. You lose control of deciding when you work, where you work, what you do, when you retire, or whether you could start your own business. Lack of freedom is a huge cost to pay to have one more garment in your closet or a few extra meals in a restaurant.

2. When you spend, you end up with "stuff." The stuff is just as imprisoning as debt. You spend your time buying

stuff. You spend your time fixing it. You feel time pressure to use it. You feel guilt when you see the stuff not used and the money wasted. Above all, the stuff will not make you happy. Too many of us spend our time buying what we don't want, to impress people we don't like, with money we don't have. What you really wanted to buy is not for sale. They don't sell contentment in a store.

3. When and if you get around to thinking about investing, you're in a hurry. You want the investment result just as quickly as you buy a car. The result is almost always an investment of high risk. You will likely be investing with borrowed money. This adds up to a perfect recipe to lose your capital, and you could end up even further in debt.

The book *Your Money or Your Life* takes you through an exercise that forces you to measure how many hours of your time you must invest to buy an item. This exercise of tying time to purchases is very useful. You quickly realize that all your time is being spent so you can buy the stuff.

The authors introduce the concept of "enough." Once you have assessed your priorities, you will find some things that you need and some things that you want. Usually the amount of both things is significantly less than what you have now. Getting control of what is enough is very liberating. It can provide you with a value system for more than just what you will purchase. It provides a value system for your life and allows you to focus on your purpose in life.

As an example, I would like to share my purpose in life. This is an entirely personal point of view and may not have any value to you other than as an example of a value system. The method by which I judge the success of my life consists of three factors:

1. The love I have shared.
2. The teaching I have done.
3. The service I have given.

None of these deals with what I own or what my net worth may be, but examining them certainly can help me assign a value to things when it is time to make decisions. These decisions may be small decisions like getting a new jacket or major decisions like pursuing a new career.

You may think this is getting a little heavy. All you wanted to do was save a little money, not make the world a better place. Unfortunately, unless you have a perspective of your life, you will never be able to effectively put money into it. You will either master your life and your money or the earning and spending of money will master you. You are not your income. You are not your net worth. And you are not what you own. Knowing what and who you are will give you perspective.

SAVERS

So who are savers? They do not look all that different from spenders at first glance. Indeed, the differences are sometimes subtle.

This subtle difference was best summarized by Charles Dickens in *David Copperfield*. Mr. Micawber says to David, "Annual income twenty pounds, annual expenditure nineteen, nineteen and six, result happiness. Annual income twenty pounds, annual expenditure twenty pounds ought and six, result misery."

Although incomes today are significantly higher than twenty pounds, nothing else has changed in this statement. The same principles we talked about in Green still apply. Make sure you set aside your savings first, then you can spend the rest. Don't buy more than you can afford. The financial benefits of saving are obvious. However, the real magic comes in the enhanced self-confidence you gain and the contentment of increasing your control over your life.

Dr. Thomas Stanley has researched the spending habits, attitudes, and lifestyle of the average millionaire. The results were quite surprising. I have summarized some of his findings:

- The average age of a millionaire is fifty-seven.
- Eighty percent of them are first-generation millionaires.
- They don't feel rich and don't flaunt their wealth.
- They are frugal bargain hunters.
- They drive older American cars.
- They dress moderately and conservatively.
- Most live in middle-class neighbourhoods.
- They are independent thinkers who believe in their own decision-making abilities.
- They are paid for performance and are generally self-employed.
- They do not like paying taxes.

Millionaires don't display the characteristics of spenders. Millionaires display the characteristics of savers. Go back and read the list of saving ideas in Green. Most millionaires could have put together this list and added many more items.

ENTREPRENEURS

Many people who become millionaires are entrepreneurs. Today, being regarded as an entrepreneur has attained glamour status. But what does it take to be an entrepreneur? Do you have these qualities?

- Are you self-reliant and have faith in your own opinions?
- Are you independent?
- Are you action oriented?
- Do you see the business as a way of serving customers at a profit?
- Can you counter your fears with courage and confidence?
- Can you focus on success and not failure?
- Are you motivated by challenge and focused on creating something from nothing?
- Do you require money incentives to make you work hard?
- Do you feel fenced in by bureaucracy and passionately need to do it your way?

If you answered yes to these questions, you have the personality and attitudes of an entrepreneur. Just because you own a business does not make you an entrepreneur. Gamblers and spenders can own a business too. The difference between the two is that the gamblers and spenders will be focusing on the payoff. The entrepreneur will focus on the process. The entrepreneur will not only delay the payoff, but will constantly reinvest it to expand the enterprise. The business will get bigger and more successful. The gambler and spender will quickly take out any profit and flaunt it in an enhanced lifestyle only to eventually cause the business to go broke or damage it severely.

The spender and gambler bring a get-rich-quick attitude, which has not proven to be helpful in building a business. Ultimately, the same principles that we presented in Purple and Green apply here. If you find something you can be absorbed by and stick to it for five, ten, or twenty years, you might end up with a very successful business and become a millionaire. You are going to have to be completely involved in this business for a long period of time. Do your research. Don't jump at every opportunity. *Never* think that this is a once-in-a-lifetime oppor-tunity. Walk confidently towards an opportunity that lets you expand your involvement in a field of great interest to you. You can't copy anyone else, just follow your own passions.

Sometimes, people who are interested in owning a business miss some of the best opportunities by assuming they have to start it themselves. You can buy an existing business. Actually, many excellent businesses are available for sale at all times. Not all of them will be right for you, but do not overlook their pos-sibilities. You can often buy the assets of an existing business at below replacement cost. You get existing customers and employees as well as systems and a cash flow. These are things a bank needs to see if it is going to provide financing. A banker will not respond well to your version of "I have a dream."

One of the added bonuses of buying an existing business is that it comes with an established customer base, so the business has money flowing into it when you purchase it. This income can help you pay for the business. The assets can be used as col-lateral for a loan. In most cases, the person selling you the business takes back most of the financing. You can usually get more favourable borrowing terms from the seller than from a financial institution. Typically, these sales involve a 25% cash down payment and financing of the other 75%, which is paid back out of earnings over a five- to seven-year time frame.

The best business to buy is one about which you have knowl-edge, experience, and passion. Look for a business where the owner is between the ages of fifty-five and sixty-five and who has owned the business for over fifteen years. The business should have little or no debt, but earnings are not growing because the owner has lost interest. The business should be in an industry that is established and is growing. Ideally, the business will have a niche market.

It is paramount that you remember the walk-don't-run credo. Don't rush into *any* deal. The secret to success is often found more in what you say no to than what you say yes to.

Where do you look for these deals? The best place is one with which you are personally familiar. You may work there, or it may be a customer or supplier of your present employer. In addition, accountants, lawyers, and financial planners are often aware of potential opportunities. Although there are brokers who are involved in marketing businesses, your best deal could be with an owner who has not figured out his or her own exit strategy until you show up. Just ask the owner if you could buy the business. The normal rules of bargaining apply. Don't show all your cards too soon, and don't appear to be in a hurry.

Running a business takes three basic skills. The first, and usually the most important, is selling and marketing. No customers means no business. The second is delivering your product or service. Third is administration and accounting. Income must exceed expenses. Assess your own skills in these three areas. Once you've identified the tasks you are most skilled at, decide if you can hire staff to do the rest. If you don't have some skills in sales and marketing, you had better think again. Some things simply cannot be delegated, at least in the beginning.

Being an entrepreneur is not all roses. Ninety percent of all companies fail. Many people don't like the job once they have it. The glamour wears off quickly, but the pressure and the day-to-day drudgery do not. That is why you had better be passionate about a business. Most people don't realize that as the owner they will have to perform many tasks, not only the ones they like but also the ones they do not. People coming from big companies will be used to a situation in which they could specialize in the things they liked while someone else did the rest. Most people prefer this structure. They also prefer a regular paycheque. They like going home at night and on the weekend knowing that the job can be left behind. As an employee, all you can lose is your job. For an entrepreneur, everything is on the line all the time.

Even if you don't want to be an entrepreneur, you will need to adopt some of the entrepreneurial attitudes listed earlier. Most new job opportunities are being created by small entrepreneurial companies.

Since 1990, employment in the public service has declined. Employment in private companies has been flat, with big companies declining and little companies expanding. Self-employment is skyrocketing.

This age of the entrepreneur is not a fad. It will not go away. Contract employment — essentially self-employment — is a growing trend. You will have to market yourself as a business. You may be the only employee and the only asset will be your skill and the value you can bring to your customer, who may be the federal government or your neighbour.

To be successful at marketing yourself, focus your business. Know your product and your customer. Be prepared to sell your service. Develop your network. Don't wait for the phone to ring. Take a positive attitude towards your personal growth.

Finally, remember to set goals. Putting them down in writing is essential. Base them on a three-year time frame, a period that is long enough for you to visualize a different set of circumstances, but soon enough for you to implement the required changes. In the words of Ralph Waldo Emerson, "The world makes way for the man who knows where he is going."

ADVISERS

So how are we doing on those finances? Have you got that debt under control? The process of building your financial plan will

Canada's Changing Employment Picture

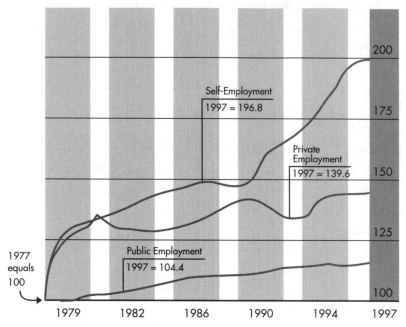

Source: Statistics Canada, 1997 data as at July (seasonally adjusted)

need help. You will need a lawyer for your will. You may need someone to help with the business accounting and with taxes. In addition, you will need someone to educate you on all the options for investing and insurance.

Choosing these people is not easy. The following guidelines may help in choosing your financial adviser:

- Ask friends and family for recommendations.
- Ask potential advisers about their experience and their professional qualifications.
- Find out if they are licensed to sell mutual funds, securities, or insurance.
- Ask if they are independent or are tied to a specific firm.

- Only accept someone you are comfortable with and trust.
- Outline the role you expect them to play and how often you wish to communicate with them.
- Discuss your rate-of-return expectations and the time frame over which you would like to invest.
- After choosing an adviser, make sure you provide him or her with all relevant information. This includes revealing your income, assets, liabilities, family obligations, potential inheritances, and even your age. Otherwise, he or she will not be able to give you advice that is appropriate to you.

WILLS

One of your early priorities is to make a will. Preparing a will can save your heirs time, money, and aggravation. If you don't have a will, critical decisions about your assets are going to be made by others or in accordance with government rules of intestacy. Here are a few of the basics you need to know about a will:

- Choose an executor. The executor receives authority from your will to act immediately after your death to fulfill the wishes expressed in your will. If you die intestate, no one is empowered to deal with your assets until an appointment has been made by the court. The person so designated may not be the most capable to deal with your estate.
- Your will directs how your property is to be distributed. If you die intestate, provincial law prescribes not only the persons who are entitled to share in your estate but also what their share is.
- Your will may reflect tax planning alternatives available to you. For example, you may leave certain assets to a

spouse or a spousal trust to defer capital gains tax on your death. You may establish one or more trusts.

• You can designate substitute executors in the event your chosen executor is unable to act or to continue to act.

While you are setting up your will, you should create a power of attorney for financial matters in the event of your incapacity. This document transfers authority over your affairs to the person of your choice, who can sign documents, pay bills, and handle other financial matters on your behalf. If this document is not created in advance, your affairs could be paralyzed until the government appoints a trustee, a costly and time-consuming undertaking. It may also result in a person not of your choosing being appointed.

INCOME TAX

Income taxes are one of those certainties we all live with. Knowing how the tax system works can have significant benefits to you, all of which you are entitled to but which can be lost if you don't know about them. Here are three ways to learn about taxes:

• Buy an income tax program for your home computer (these programs cost less than $50). This will allow you to preview or even complete your own tax return. It will let you do some tax planning scenarios. For example, you can see how much tax you would save with an RRSP contribution, or if through your business you were able to split income with a spouse to lower your overall tax rate. The programs also have very good Help menus that explain most tax issues.

- All major bookstores carry many good tax preparation books, including those by Evelyn Jacks on tax-reducing ideas.
- Get a tax specialist to work with you. It costs money, but these specialists will save you more in taxes than they cost. If you are to be audited, you will be very happy to have them in your corner. Revenue Canada can be an intimidating opponent. After all, they know the rules and you don't. It will be your money on the table, and they want it.

The most important thing to understand about income tax is that you pay a higher rate of tax as your income goes up. The second key issue is that you pay a different level of tax for different types of income. Income from salary or interest is taxed higher than income from dividends or capital gains. These two points are critical because they significantly affect your investment strategies.

Most tax planning strategies are based on an understanding of the information in the chart below.

INCOME LEVEL	SALARY AND INTEREST INCOME TAX RATE	CAPITAL GAIN (75% TAXABLE) TAX RATE	DIVIDEND INCOME TAX RATE
$0–29,590	27%	20%	7%
$29,591–59,180	41%	25%	25%
$59,181 and up	50%	37%	33%

These tax rates are approximate and vary by province. Just remember, higher income is taxed at a higher rate, and not all income sources are taxed the same.

It's Not What You Get, It's What You Net!

Top Marginal Provincial Tax Rates

British Columbia	54.17%	P.E.I.	50.30%
Newfoundland	53.33%	Nova Scotia	49.98%
Quebec	53.02%	Yukon	46.55%
Saskatchewan	51.95%	Non-Resident	46.40%
Ontario	51.64%	Alberta	46.07%
New Brunswick	51.05%	N.W.T.	44.37%
Manitoba	50.40%		

Source: Deloitte & Touche

After-Tax Yield of Investments

	Before-Tax Yield	After-Tax Yield	Effective Tax Rate
Dividends	10.00%	7.06%	29.38%
Interest	10.00%	5.65%	43.50%
Capital Gains	10.00%	6.74%	32.63%

Figures for an individual resident in Canada at ot near the top federal tax rate in 1997 and a basic provincial tax rate of 50%. They do not take into account any provincial or federal surtaxes that may apply. Figures will vary from province to province.

RRSPs

There are two key ways to invest: Inside a registered retirement savings plan (RRSP) and outside. Money held in an RRSP is not taxed until it comes out of the plan; then it is all taxed at the same rate as salary or interest income. Investments held outside an RRSP are taxed differently. The effect of these taxes is shown in the above chart discussing after-tax yield of investments.

An RRSP has two huge advantages that make it an essential part of all Canadians' savings programs.

1. You are able to deduct your RRSP contribution from current taxable income. You pay tax only when you take the money out years later, when you may be in a lower tax bracket.
2. The growth of the capital inside an RRSP is not taxable each year. You pay tax on the growth only when the money comes out. The money can be taken out slowly over many years in retirement, which further defers the income taxes due on this money.

It is the combination of these two tax issues that make RRSPs an essential part of your investment strategy. The accompanying chart indicates how much of your income you need to save to reach 70% of your preretirement income, which experts suggest you need to maintain your lifestyle. They also make it painfully obvious why you need to start contributing early and why using an RRSP makes so much sense.

There are many other key issues that you should focus on in order to maximize the growth of your RRSP.

• Make your annual contribution early in the year rather than waiting until the last minute. This will effectively give one more year of compounding and over time this makes a big difference.

• Always try to make your maximum contribution. The limit is 18% of your eligible income from the previous tax year to a maximum of $13,500. When you get an assessment notice from Revenue Canada acknowledging your tax return has been reviewed, it shows the amount you can contribute to your next year's RRSP. It also includes the amount of unused contributions from previous years. Try to keep fully contributed at all times.

- Setting up an automatic monthly contribution is an excellent idea. This can be done on your own or through a group RRSP at work. Not only can you take advantage of early contributions, but it provides you with a more disciplined approach to making the contribution. This method also allows you to take advantage of dollar-cost averaging with equity investments. When prices are down one month, your regular contribution will buy more units of the investment. When prices are up, it will buy fewer units. This is a built-in strategy to allow you to buy low and sell high. It also takes away the anxiety of trying to time the market with your annual contribution.

- A case can be made for borrowing to contribute to an RRSP or to make RRSP catch-up deposits. It is critical that you use any tax savings to pay off part of the debt and that you have a structured repayment schedule for the balance. If you spend the tax savings and don't make an effort to quickly pay off this loan, then all you have done is added to your debt problems.

- Use inheritances, severance payments, or any other large sum of money made available to you to make catch-up contributions.

- If you are married, name your spouse as your beneficiary. Upon death, all RRSPs can be rolled over to a spouse without attracting tax. The money is still in an RRSP for your spouse and will be taxed only when he or she takes the money out.

- If your spouse has a lower income than you or has fewer savings to provide him or her with a retirement income,

How much money do you need to save to receive 70% of your present income upon retirement?

Required Percentage of Salary That Must Be Saved Using RRSPs to Achieve 70% Integrated Replacement Ratio

	Age at which saving starts	Age at retirement 60	Age at retirement 65
Men	25	8.9	6.4
	35	13.6	9.4
	45	24.7	15.3
Women	25	10.3	7.6
	35	15.7	11.1
	45	28.5	18.1

Source: Dr. Robert L. Brown, Economic Security in an Aging Population.

pay your contribution into a spousal RRSP plan. The goal is to equalize your incomes in retirement and minimize taxes at that time.

- Have a diversified portfolio of investments in your RRSP. Take advantage of some more volatile types of investments that have the potential for much higher returns.

- Use the full 20% foreign content allowed. After all, Canada represents less than 3% of world equity markets. Don't ignore the opportunities that can be found in the other 97% of the world.

- Consider your RRSP as a part of your overall investment strategy. Some investments, such as real estate, can't be held in an RRSP. Interest income is sheltered inside an RRSP but fully taxable outside. Capital gains receive somewhat more favourable treatment outside an RRSP.

Market volatility is your friend
with dollar cost averaging!

Monthly Contribution	Unit Value	Units Purchased	Total Units Owned
$100	10.00	10	10
100	9.09	11	21
100	8.33	12	33
100	9.09	11	44
100	11.11	9	53
100	10.00	10	63

Total Contribution =	6 x $100	= $600
Market Value =	63 units x $10	= $630
Capital Gain		= $30

If the $600 was used to purchase all sixty units in the beginning, it would still be worth $600.

Despite all these overwhelming reasons for having an RRSP, 60% of all tax filers do not make RRSP contributions and only 11% of them make their maximum RRSP contribution. The very best advice anywhere in this book is this: Put as much as you can into an RRSP and as soon as you can. Then leave it there.

BUYING A HOME

The big debate people often face when planning their finances is between buying a house and starting an RRSP. Home ownership has many advantages. The most obvious is that you can live there. You have to live somewhere, and if you do not own, you have to pay rent. The second major advantage is that if the value of your principal residence goes up, you do not pay tax on the gain when you sell. One disadvantage is that interest paid for a home mortgage is not deductible from taxes, so you are paying this interest with after-tax dollars. Some people try to combine these two objectives by using a loan from their RRSP to help buy their home.

I have seen many mathematical calculations trying to prove whether it is better to put money into an RRSP or pay off a mortgage. Everyone is entitled to an opinion. My opinion is an RRSP is a pension plan. It will provide you and your family with long-term financial security. This should be your number one priority. You can rent or purchase housing that fits your budget. Buying or renting more luxurious accommodation is a lifestyle decision.

I am not a fan of Ottawa's RRSP Home Buyers Plan. This allows you to borrow money from your RRSP to help purchase a home. Human nature is such that you think you are getting better housing today *and* saving for retirement. In fact, you are allowed to borrow up to $20,000 from your RRSP. You do not have to pay any interest, but must pay the principal back to your RRSP in fifteen years. This seems attractive, until you consider the impact on your RRSP. Applying the Rule of 72, calculate that at a 10% return, your RRSP could have almost doubled twice to approximately $80,000 during that fifteen years. A better lifestyle today is a powerful motivator in our society, but an RRSP should always be considered a "no-touch" account.

Once you have looked after your RRSP, you can allocate whatever money you wish to improving your accommodation. Most of us have not followed this advice. Ask yourself this question: Is the extra pleasure of a better home now worth having less financial freedom in the future?

I can hear some of you screaming, "My house will be worth a whole lot more when I retire." I am sure you have heard the warnings of David Foot in his book *Boom, Bust & Echo*. He has said that housing prices will decline as the baby boomers pass the period in their lives when they buy houses. In the near future, there will be more boomers selling homes than buying them. I think this may be too simplistic. I think real estate value is based on location, location, location. Some housing will keep going up in value. Some will not. Overall, the guaranteed growth of the 1970s and 1980s is gone, so unless you are planning to completely change your life and relocate from a community of high housing costs to one of low housing costs, don't count on your house as a retirement plan. Put your money into your RRSP first, then pay off your mortgage as fast as possible. Interest paid on a home mortgage is not deductible from your income for tax purposes. Paying off non-deductible debt becomes a great investment strategy.

FINANCING A HOME

When you are financing your home, what interest period should you take? No one has a crystal ball to be able to predict what interest rates are going to do. I believe that you are always best to borrow short term but establish your mortgage payments at more than the minimum. This gives you a cushion if interest rates happen to have gone up when you renew your mortgage. If they stay at the same levels, you will be paying off the mortgage even faster. For example, on a $100,000 mortgage, if you choose a one-year interest term at 5.5%, you will pay $610 a month. For a five-year term at 7%, the monthly payment is $700. By choosing the one-year term at a rate of 5.5% and making your monthly payment $700, you would be paying an extra $90 monthly against the principal. This pays off the mortgage in nineteen years, not twenty-five.

There are many other strategies to help you pay down your mortgage more quickly. By paying weekly and not monthly, you make the equivalent of one extra payment a year. Use the tax refund from your RRSP contribution to pay down the mortgage too. Normally you can pay off up to 10% of a mortgage each year without a penalty.

Owning a home has proven to be a good investment, partly because you are forcing yourself in effect to "save" a little money each month by making the mortgage payment. You "save" this money whether you want to or not. Try to avoid refinancing your home unless it is for necessary renovations. Once you reach Silver, you may wish to consider borrowing against your home as a reverse mortgage. Prior to that, resist the temptation.

Home ownership has one other major benefit. The increase in the value of the home is not a taxable gain when you come to sell. In the past, when house prices have risen sharply, this has been a huge benefit. Today, though, stable house prices have removed some of the temptation to buy the biggest house you can possibly afford and let inflation bail you out with a big non-taxable profit when you sell.

Unless you are in the business of renovating run-down homes and reselling them, you should try to limit the number of times you buy and sell. Moving is expensive. The cost of the realtor, the lawyer, the mover, the tax man, and the decorator all add up. As well, your old furniture is never quite right. With all these costs, and the time and energy involved, it is hard to imagine you have gained anything.

CONTINUING EDUCATION

The federal government provides another temptation to use your RRSP funds prior to retirement. Adults who want to return to school are allowed to borrow up to $10,000 a year free from their RRSPs to a maximum of $20,000 over a four-year period. All withdrawals must be paid back in ten years. Continuing education and retraining are necessary and critically important priorities, but I encourage you to exhaust every other financial source before you take money away from your future pension. Remember, when you are using the money, it is not growing.

CHOOSING YOUR INVESTMENTS

Before you make any investments, ask yourself these questions:

- Do you have any expertise? Do you know anything about stocks, bonds, or real estate?
- Do you want to spend your time learning about investments? Do you want to spend your time working on your investments?
- Are you prepared to keep track of all the aspects of your investments, including tax implications?
- Do you have a trustworthy adviser to work with?
- What level of risk are you prepared to live with? Most Canadians don't like risk. Are you sure you are the exception?
- Do you have a plan, a clear idea of what you are trying to accomplish? Do you have a realistic time frame to do it in? Wanting more as soon as possible is not a strategy.

Some of the most difficult challenges with investing involve mastering your own emotions. When people are optimistic about the future, all their money becomes risk capital. When something goes wrong, they become pessimistic about the future and none of their money is risk capital. They want everything back in the savings account as soon as possible. Having a plan, having an adviser, and knowing yourself can allow you to overcome this reaction.

When the famous investor J. P. Morgan was asked his prediction on the markets, he said, "They will continue to fluctuate." That they have, and that they will. This includes the market for stocks, bonds, real estate, gold, gems, art, or anything else you can think of investing in.

Diversifying is the way to live with fluctuations in the market. Sam Snead's description of golf applies just as well to investing: "The sun don't shine on the same dog's back all the time." You will want to have some of your assets in a variety of investment classes.

A diversified investment portfolio is like an eight-cylinder engine. Each cylinder represents a different class of investments. Just like an engine, all the pistons will not be at the top at the same time. More importantly, they will not all be at the bottom at the same time. Some will be up and some down at all times. The important thing for you is to ignore the individual cylinders and focus on what the engine is doing. Hopefully, it is moving you forward in the direction of your financial goals, which in most cases would include a well-funded retirement, an education fund for your children, and the emotional freedom that comes with financial independence.

MUTUAL FUNDS

"What are mutual funds and why should I use them?" Good question. There are well over 1,000 mutual funds in Canada. They come in all shapes and sizes. Mutual funds are products that allow individuals access to professional money management at a low cost. No matter what type of mutual fund you purchase, the professional managers continually search for good investments and monitor the performance of the fund relative to the stated objectives of the fund. A level of diversification is built into the mandate of every fund regarding what can be owned by the fund and how concentrated it can be in any one investment.

Mutual funds provide a liquid investment. They do not guarantee your original investment, but knowing you can get your cash out at any time is a very important option. Mutual funds can be purchased in large or small sums. You can also choose to make monthly payments automatically from your bank account. Mutual fund companies provide good reporting on your investment and all the relevant information for tax filing. Mutual funds that invest in equities can have capital gains on which the tax is deferred until the stocks are sold. This combination of benefits has made mutual funds the investment of choice for most people in recent years.

When the eight-cylinder engine theory of diversification is applied to mutual funds, it looks like this:

The first cylinder of the engine is money market funds. These provide interest income only and your original capital is not at risk. There is no chance of a capital gain. These are very conservative funds.

In the second cylinder are Canadian fixed income funds, international fixed income funds, and mortgage funds. These primarily produce interest income. Some of them are able to complement interest income with some capital gains as the manager selects different time frames in which to invest to take advantage of interest rate fluctuations. All these funds are generally considered conservative but have had some big swings when interest rates change rapidly. These funds go up in value when interest rates go down and go down in value when interest rates go up.

The third cylinder contains Canadian blue-chip equity funds. These funds own shares in Canada's biggest and best companies. They will reflect the current attitude of investors to the Canadian economy. Most experts feel Canada will do very well over the next decade as our governments continue to gain control of their debt and world economies are expanding, creating a need for

Diversification

The Eight Cylinders of Mutual Fund Investing

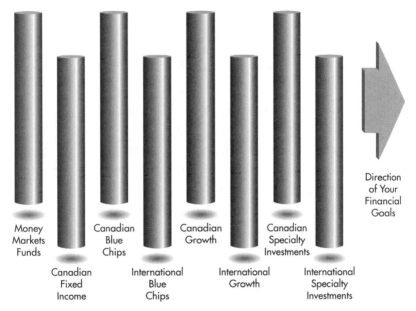

Money
Markets
Funds

Canadian
Fixed
Income

Canadian
Blue
Chips

International
Blue
Chips

Canadian
Growth

International
Growth

Canadian
Specialty
Investments

International
Specialty
Investments

Direction
of Your
Financial
Goals

our natural resources. These funds are considered moderately conservative. Dividend funds are the most conservative Canadian equity funds. These funds produce some dividend income, which has favoured tax treatment when the investment is not in an RRSP.

The fourth cylinder contains the large company global funds. These funds invest in the best companies in the world, whether they are in North America, Europe, Japan, or elsewhere. The manager typically will put varying emphasis on each of these markets to reflect his or her opinion of future trends. These funds are also considered moderately conservative.

The fifth cylinder focuses on Canadian growth companies. These funds are more aggressive and will try to invest in companies experiencing increases in sales and profits. Many of these faster-growing companies are smaller than the typical blue-chip companies. These funds are considered more aggressive. Although they provide an opportunity for greater reward, the value of the funds will be more volatile.

The sixth cylinder will focus on the international growth companies. They are generally smaller companies in developed markets or larger companies located in less-developed markets that are experiencing rapid growth. These funds are also considered more aggressive.

The seventh cylinder has the truly aggressive funds in Canada. These funds focus on small and rapidly growing companies. Often, their value is based on a high-potential concept or a potential resource discovery. These funds could focus on specific sectors of the market, such as resources, precious metals, real estate, or technology. Their values can swing wildly but they have the potential to earn significant returns. However, you will need courage to hang on during the downs in order to catch the next big wave of growth.

The eighth cylinder contains the very aggressive international funds. They also focus on the same special sectors and rapidly growing companies. Many of these funds focus on emerging markets of the Far East or Latin America. Some focus on growth sectors such as technology and health science.

These eight cylinders represent all the different types of funds. When put together, our cylinders become a portfolio and not an engine. The makeup of your portfolio should be based on three factors: your need for growth, your investment time frames, and your comfort with risk. If you are not comfortable with investment risk or you do not need to achieve higher returns to meet your goals, your portfolio might use only the first two to four cylinders. For those who need the potentially higher returns and can accept the risk, a portfolio that uses six cylinders would be required. Normally, only individuals with a good understanding of market volatility and a longer time frame for their investments should consider using cylinders seven and eight.

In a car engine the cylinders go up and down, but you only care that the car moves forward towards a chosen destination. Similarly, a properly diversified portfolio will have different types of investments that will not go up and down at the same time. Your focus should be on reaching your financial goals and not the short-term performance of one cylinder in your portfolio. Remember, if they all go up together, they can all go down together. Few people can handle this second option.

BUILDING AN INVESTMENT PORTFOLIO

There are many theories on how to put together an investment portfolio. George Hartman's book *Risk Is a Four Letter Word* provides an excellent education. It is an understandable guide to setting up a portfolio and it is focused on the needs of Canadians.

Investing is about risk and return. Take a look at the illustration on page 86. The vertical axis represents a rate of return. The horizontal axis represents risk.

If you were to pick the ideal investment, you would choose investment A. High return and no risk. Sorry to say, in the real world this does not exist. The worst-case scenario would be investment C, no return and high risk. In other words, you lose your money. The bad news is that in the real world, investment C is readily available. People buy investment C from someone who claims to be selling investment A. Buyer beware always applies. When someone is offering you a "chance of a lifetime" or a "no risk, high return" investment, ask yourself the following question: "If this investment is so good, why do they need me?" You will quickly realize that if it were that good, they would be keeping it to themselves and not selling it to you.

Buyer Beware

If It Sounds Too Good To Be True, It Probably Is!

"Greed is good" may have been the motto of Gordon Gecko in the movie *Wall Street*, but in real life, greed usually leads to impatience and there is nothing more dangerous to long-term investing. The most difficult thing to do, but the most essential, is to be patient. Compound interest works, but not quickly. The old saying that "a watched pot never boils" could be easily applied to investing. It's true that you can change your life in the short term through investing — you can lose your money fast. You can't change things for the better quickly. Investing is a long-term project.

RISK VS. RETURN

Take some time studying Charts 1 and 2 and you will see the benefits of diversification. Chart 1 shows the expected risk returns of owning all bonds. Then, as you go up the curve, you

Chart 1
Combining Asset Classes
May Increase Return Without Adding Risk
Higher Returns Without Adding Risk
Since Inception of the TSE Total Return Index

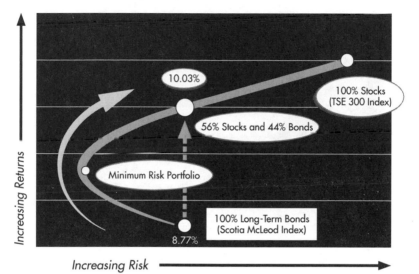

Historically, a portfolio that combined 56% stocks and 44% bonds would have increased average annual returns by more than 1.2% without adding any more risk.

Data Source: Ibbotson

see the benefit of adding stocks. Voilà. You now see how diversification with different asset classes can reduce risk and increase return at the same time.

In Chart 2, you can see the risk-return characteristics of having only stocks on the Toronto Stock Exchange. The chart shows that you can have higher returns and lower risk by adding some international stocks. Eventually, with more international stocks, the potential returns keep growing but the risk stops decreasing and starts to increase. The risk eventually becomes the same as investing only in the TSE and ultimately becomes higher. Most people want to end up in that higher-return and

Chart 2
Combining International and Canadian Stocks
May Increase Return Without Adding Risk

Benefit from International Diversification
25-Year Historical Annual Results from 1970

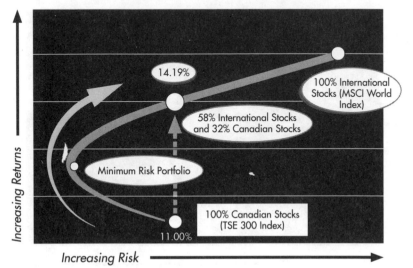

Historically, a portfolio that combined 68% international stocks with
32% Canadian stocks would have increased average annual returns by
more than 3% without adding any more risk.

Data Source: Ibbotson

lower-risk area. This is why you should always have the maximum 20% foreign content in your RRSP.

At the risk of oversimplifying a complex topic, let me introduce one more of my favourite analogies. I call this the birthday
cake theory of diversification. It deals with that critical factor of
emotions. It can help you prepare to meet both your greed and
your fear.

First, you start out with the cake. This is the part of your portfolio with which you are not prepared to take too many chances.
For many people, all they want is cake. The cake contains the
more conservative funds found in the first four cylinders we

talked about earlier. If the fear of loss is overpowering, you should own only cake.

If you vacillate between fear and greed, you will need some icing. The icing funds are found in cylinders five and six of the mutual fund scenario. When things go well, you want to know you are participating in that growth. When they go badly, you want to know that most of your money is in the cake funds.

Then we have our candle funds. These are in cylinders seven and eight. When stock markets are soaring, we want to brag that we are sharing in the bonanza. We love to boast to our buddies how we had a fund that made mega returns this year. How much of these you can handle is determined only when the market goes in the tank, and you are gripped with fear. If you can reach your goals without these more volatile funds or if you are at an older age where you cannot accept a loss, you should not have any of these funds. However, if knowing that the bulk of your money is in the cake and icing funds gives you the confidence to hang on to your candle funds throughout their roller-coaster ride, you will likely be well rewarded in the long term. I suggest having no more than 5 to 10% of your money in these candle funds.

GUARANTEED INVESTMENT CERTIFICATES (GICs)

A Guaranteed Investment Certificate (GIC) provides a no-risk method of investing. The interest rate is guaranteed for a preset period of time, usually one to five years. GICs are available from most financial institutions.

The guaranteed investment certificate is a popular investment, but lower interest rates have reduced the demand for this product. However, many financial institutions are coming up with new and creative ways to package them. History has generally proven that taking the higher rates on a longer term is better when purchasing GICs or similar interest-bearing products.

The safety of their money is very important to GIC investors. Many of these people consciously place their money with a variety of financial institutions in order to avoid having more than $60,000 in any one institution. This is the amount protected by government deposit insurance.

WHO NEEDS AN ADVISER?

I have a very unscientific perspective on people and their money and investing. If you have a group of a hundred people, all in the Red stage of life, fifty have no money. These people should start a monthly savings plan as soon as possible. Don't worry too much about what investment you choose until you have a few thousand saved.

At the other end of the scale are ten people who, though they don't necessarily have the most money, want to take a very active interest in the investing of their money. They are usually best suited to investing in commercial real estate or dealing in stocks or bonds through a discount broker. A lot of what you read in the financial press is geared to selling these people advice and information. Despite their high interest in investing, they are often more vulnerable to emotional swings about where the market is going, Hand they react accordingly, usually to their own detriment.

The middle group of forty people has some money saved. They want it invested wisely. They don't want to hear about it every day. They want to spend their time running a business, being a parent, or going fishing. These people generally work with a financial adviser they trust. They take a long-term diversified approach to their investments. I believe these people not only get the best results, but also experience the least stress.

Proper Financial Advice Can Increase Your Returns

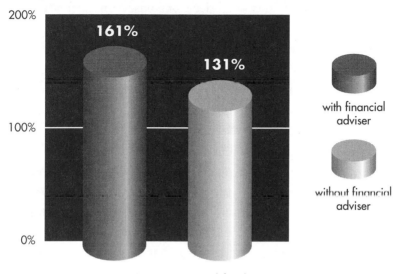

12-year mutual fund returns

Source: Dalbar Financial Services

Frankly, the people in the first group of fifty desperately need a financial adviser. Leaving it up to themselves, which is what they have done so far, simply has not worked. If you are in this group, I recommend that you take a look around. You are likely to find that your financial boat is taking on water and you need somebody to help you bail it out or it's going to sink. Get some help from an adviser now. You'll be surprised how much you accomplish in just a few years. You will have reduced your spending and built some savings. The biggest benefit will be the feeling of control over your financial life, which is a huge stress reliever.

A financial adviser will help you set your financial goals. They will help you build a plan, and will provide expertise on the investment products that will help you reach your goals while staying within your risk tolerance. The adviser will meet with you regularly to discuss your progress, and can make modifications to your plan if necessary. One of the key roles of an adviser is to help you not make emotional decisions based on market fluctuations. They will also help you maintain your long-term investment perspective.

Every athlete can benefit from having a good coach. Your financial adviser becomes your money coach. The more knowledgeable you are as an investor the more demanding your expectations will be of your financial adviser. But you will still benefit from their detached perspective and their professional advice.

Some of our ten high-involvement types will eventually realize that they are amateurs playing against professionals and are going to lose. If you're one of these, swallow your pride and get a financial adviser, then go play some golf and wonder why you wasted all that time trying to be a Warren Buffett look-alike. Some of this group will never come around and will live out their lives on the edge, biting their fingernails and getting up in the middle of the night to go on the Internet to see what the Hong Kong market is doing. Good luck — the discount brokers are counting on you guys.

TIMING THE MARKET

People who are highly involved in the stock market are the most likely to try and time the market. They believe not only that the market can be timed, despite all the research to the contrary, but that they are capable of doing it.

The market is a strange animal with its own set of emotions. At all times, some people are positive and some are negative. After all, every time a stock is bought, someone else had to sell it. When the markets go up, they are said to be climbing a "wall of worry." This probably doesn't sound like a game most people would want to participate in at all. Let me try to put things into perspective with yet another of my favourite analogies.

The Challenge of Market Timing

TSE 300 Jan. 1977–Sept. 1996	Rate of Return
Include all days	12.7%
missed 10 best days	10.0%
missed 20 best days	8.5%

I imagine a man with a yo-yo walking up a flight of stairs. Every day in the media all you hear about is the yo-yo. And over any ten-year period, you can bet that yo-yo is going to go up and down a lot. But who cares? The only thing you are really interested in is whether at the end of the ten years the man will be standing at the top of the stairs.

INVESTING LONG TERM

If I told you the TSE was going to double in the next nine years, would you care whether it was going to go up or down tomorrow? Not likely. The truth is that with our Rule of 72, we know that the market needs to get only 8% returns for nine years to double. It most likely will.

By taking a long-term perspective, you will ignore the yo-yo and focus on the man going up the stairs, which eliminates a lot of unnecessary worry. Long term should be the key to your investment strategies. The accompanying chart shows how different types of investments perform if you examine the results over time. From a one-year point of view, small-cap stocks seem to produce either a big return or a big loss. Comparatively, three-month treasury bills produce no big returns, but you can

The Benefit of Long-Term Investing
Reduction of Risk over Time

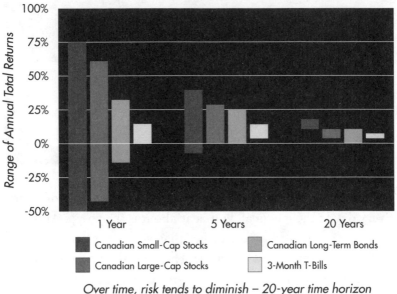

Range of Annual Total Returns

100%
75%
50%
25%
0%
-25%
-50%

1 Year   5 Years   20 Years

■ Canadian Small-Cap Stocks   ■ Canadian Long-Term Bonds

■ Canadian Large-Cap Stocks   □ 3-Month T-Bills

Over time, risk tends to diminish – 20-year time horizon
shows negative returns for any asset class.

Source: Nesbitt Burns (1969–1996), TSE 300, ScotiaMcLeod & Bank of Canada (1956–1996)

never lose money either. When we look at the results after twenty years, all the volatility of the small caps has averaged out so that the returns are more predictable. Ignoring the yo-yo will allow you to have these stocks as part of your portfolio so you can take advantage of the growth potential they offer.

Knowing how much risk you need to take is an important part of your financial planner's role. When they are provided with all the necessary information, they can show you what your present investment strategy is going to produce. They can also show you examples of what higher contributions and varying degrees of risk can do to help you reach your goal. In some cases, when people find out the amount they would need to set aside and the high degree of risk they would need to take,

Your Asset Mix
Value Today

Cash Investments

Bank Accounts and Other Cash _____

Cashable GICs _____

Term Deposits (short term) _____

Canada Savings Bonds _____

Treasury Bills _____

Money Market Mutual Funds _____

Other _____

Total Cash $ _____

Proportion of Total Assets _____ %

Income Investments

GICs _____

Bonds _____

Income Mutual Funds _____

Mortgages _____

Preferred Shares _____

Other _____

Total Income $ _____

Proportion of Total Assets _____ %

Growth Investments

Stocks _____

Equity Mutual Funds _____

Gold & Precious Metals _____

Total Growth $ _____

Proportion of Total Assets _____ %

Total Assets

they become more realistic about their goals. Others may find they do not need to expose themselves to any high risk at all.

This process of creating and implementing a plan involves the following five steps:

1. Set your financial goals. Where will you be? When will you be there? What will you be doing? What income will you need?
2. Do a full assessment of your present financial holdings. This includes a full net-worth statement and an overview of your expenses for the next year.
3. Establish a plan that can take you from where you are to where you want to go. You may want to modify your goals as you go through the planning process and realize what would be required to reach your original goals.
4. Carry out your plan. Make regular contributions to your savings. Avoid the temptation to make withdrawals.
5. Review your plan annually. This is critical. All financial plans make assumptions about interest rates, inflation, your ability to contribute, your health, your income, and your ultimate goals. All of these change. Only constant updating will keep you focused and constantly approaching your own moving target.

When setting your goals, try to keep some of these trends in mind. Life expectancy is continuing to increase. People are retiring earlier. The combination of these two events will put a lot of pressure on your pension planning. It will take more money that needs to be accumulated faster to realize your retirement dreams.

PENSIONS

Governments are going to be less helpful in the future. Income support for pensioners will decline as the number of seniors grows. The costs of medical care will continue to be transferred to the individual. Both of these policy changes increase your level of responsibility in planning your own future. Don't ignore these issues. No one else is going to look after you.

AN ENVIABLE POSITION

Some of you will be able to get to an enviable position of having your house paid for and having put the maximum you are allowed into your RRSP. Now what do you do? Some may say spend the rest of your money. Frankly, that is not a bad strategy, unless your income has significantly exceeded $90,000 per year. A person who has put the maximum into their RRSP throughout their career can generally replace about 70% of their income up to $90,000 per year. People with higher incomes will generally have to save more, maybe lots more, or else accept a substantial drop in lifestyle during retirement. If you are thinking about retiring before age sixty-five you may also need to maximize your RRSP and consider other options.

Before you spend it all, consider these other options: investing outside an RRSP, paying for a child's education, investing in commercial or residential real estate, and estate creation.

Investments outside an RRSP use the same products as those inside an RRSP, and many of the same principles still apply. The major difference involves taxation while the asset is growing. The other issue will be your need to access income, which we will deal with in Gold and beyond.

Taxation is a critical consideration. Investigate the different tax rates associated with interest, dividends, and capital gains. If possible, you would like to implement your plan for non-registered investment earnings in the following order to benefit from these different tax rates:

- The most tax-effective investment provides capital gains that can be deferred. An example would be a mutual fund you own for which the value has gone up, but the mutual fund company has not sold the shares inside the fund. Until they are sold, you don't have to declare capital gains as income. A mutual fund that commonly follows this buy-and-hold strategy is considered tax efficient. Real estate and stocks owned directly that have appreciated over time also benefits from this deferral of capital gains.
- Try to earn dividends from either common or preferred shares that qualify for the dividend tax credit.
- Only 75% of a realized capital gain is taxable.
- Rental income is fully taxable but does allow for the deduction of expenses and for the depreciation on the building, which lowers the taxable income you receive on rental properties.
- Interest income is fully exposed to income tax yearly. This is the least attractive option from a tax point of view but these are usually less risky investments.

Remember: taxation is not always the most important consideration in financial planning. In addition, it's essential to assess your comfort level with risk before you make any investments. This is particularly true if someone is selling you a product as a tax shelter. Your accountant can provide the necessary independent advice before proceeding.

EDUCATION FUNDS

Way back in White we talked about how wonderful it would be if your parents (or grandparents) contributed to an education fund on your behalf.

This idea sounded a lot more exciting when you were the potential recipient than it does now when you might be the contributor. Regardless of your perspective, it does not change the fact that kids need an education and that it costs a lot of money to get it.

As in most situations, pay a little now or a lot later. The best way to approach this reality is to set money aside on a regular basis from the time the child is very young. The longer your time frame, the more manageable the problem. We talked about a few methods in White but the most common were an in-trust account with a mutual fund company or an RESP. Annual RESP contributions up to $2,000 now qualify for a 20% grant from the federal government. This can mean up to an additional $400 each year.

REAL ESTATE

Real estate can be a very good investment. Commercial real estate investing, however, is not for amateurs. Most people have no idea of the costs associated with ownership. Some of the costs are taxes, utilities, maintenance, legal fees, vacancy, real estate commissions, and insurance. If you are able to commit considerable time to managing these properties and you have the skill to do many of the repairs, it may be a good alternative for you. Otherwise, stay away. Real estate also fails a key test for any individual investor: it is not always liquid. Just because you want or need the money doesn't mean someone will want to buy your property at your price when you want them to. Under no condition should you get involved in real estate as an investment if you plan to own it for less than ten years.

Some people regard the purchase of recreational property as an investment. It is true that most property values go up over time. However, if property taxes, maintenance, carrying costs, and condo fees are all considered, over a period of ten to twenty years you would usually be ahead financially if you rent accommodation for vacations rather than own recreational property. Your capital can then be invested in a more traditional, and a more liquid, investment. If a recreational property is your lifestyle choice, enjoy it, but don't try to justify the decision as an investment.

INHERITANCES

Now let's talk about inheritances. If you inherit money, make sure it doesn't go to your head. You did not earn this money. Being born on third base is not the same as hitting a triple. This is a one-time deal, not to be repeated. Make sure you plan how this asset is going to help you accomplish all the things you want it to do over time. Try using the money the way the person who gave it to you might have done. He or she was the one who saved it and likely had a pretty good handle on how to keep it. Start putting into practice the statement that "thrift is an admirable quality, particularly in an ancestor." Don't forget that you are the ancestor to your heirs.

Once you know you are going to get an inheritance, you have plans to make. The larger the amount, the more planning necessary. It is always wise to seek the help of your adviser. Consider marital stability before you allocate the assets. The advice that follows assumes divorce is not an issue.

- Don't make your inheritance public knowledge.
- Ask yourself if you need to revise your own will or estate plan.

- When the money arrives, don't spend it. Put it in a term deposit for thirty days.
- Decide if you want the amount of your inheritance passed down to your children. If you do, set aside a small portion of the inheritance to prepay the premiums on a permanent life insurance policy in that amount. This leaves you free to do as you wish with the rest of the money. Your insurance adviser can help you structure this to avoid or minimize taxes. The death benefit is directed to your kids tax-free and your inheritance is perpetuated. Life insurance proceeds pass to your estate without probate fees. Life insurance assets are protected from your creditors and they can help solve family law implications involving marriage or remarriage.
- Use the next portion of your inheritance to pay off non-deductible interest loans. Visa and other credit cards should be eliminated first, then other personal loans and car loans, and, finally, mortgages.
- Contribute to your RRSP, including all catch-up privileges. Consider a spousal RRSP.
- Set up educational trust accounts for each child or grand-child.
- Re-assess your ability to meet long-term financial goals. To what degree is the inheritance necessary to help you do this? Set up a tax-efficient investment account that can make your long-term goals become a reality.
- If you have done all of these, keep a few things in mind before you spend the rest of the money. First, many assets that you can purchase with the inheritance may bring added ongoing operational costs to you, such as those associated with buying a boat. Second, remember that assets that appreciate are better than ones that do not.

INSURANCE

So, what's left to do financially in Red? Just the same old basics of life insurance and disability insurance.

These are the critical years for life insurance. All those dreams you have for your family are conditional on your being here and earning the money. Do your best to make sure that if you die, your family still has a chance to achieve the essentials of that dream. Consider the following issues:

- Both spouses should have their insurance needs assessed.
- Insurance should provide for all debts and mortgages, education costs, and any liabilities that your death may create, such as funeral costs, legal costs, capital gains taxes, or an RRSP that becomes taxable when both spouses die.
- In addition, enough capital should exist to replace your income in the future. This income is normally recommended to be at least 70% of what your earnings are today. Allow for inflation. Most people are surprised at the large amount of capital necessary to replace their income. It's better that you are surprised now than that your family is later. To replace 70% of a $50,000-a-year income, assuming a 5% after-tax return and no inflation, would require $700,000 of income. Add your debts to this amount. The total goes up quickly if you make adjustments for inflation.
- Realistically, few people have a choice other than to use term insurance to cover the major part of their needs, though many people will have some group insurance at work. Your group insurance should be a supplement to your personally owned life insurance. With high unemployment, frequent career changes, and increasing reliance on self-employment, you cannot afford to have only group

insurance. You may end up between jobs with no coverage and be unable to be insured because of health changes.

- There will always be a need for some tax-free liquid capital at death. To meet this need you would be wise to own some of your insurance on a permanent basis. The initial premiums for this coverage are higher but they do not increase. You should be aware that there are attractive tax-effective benefits for the cash-value growth in these policies. Good advice will be essential in setting this up.

Disability insurance is particularly important in the Red stage. Disability is statistically much more likely to occur than death. You need to be able to replace about 60% of your income through disability insurance. Some people will have coverage through their place of employment; some will have to top up what they have at work with a personal plan.

The benefits from the best disability plans would start paying you a non-taxable income after 90 days. The payments would continue until age sixty-five. Your income dictates the maximum amount of disability insurance you can purchase. However, you may apply to have your coverage increase as your income increases. The premiums for personally owned disability insurance are paid with after-tax dollars.

If your company is paying for your disability insurance, the benefit is taxable, so you will need even more coverage to pay the taxes.

As mentioned in Green, disability and life insurance are definitely not an option. They may not be your favourite place to allocate money, but they are something you must have.

LOOKING BACK

At the end of Red you want to know that you have experienced life. You have had accomplishments and you have had failures. You have learned and you have matured. Ambition has been overtaken by acceptance. Some relationships have survived the test of time. New relationships will have to be created for tomorrow. If you have graduated from being a spender, you will be leaving Red with more memories than stuff.

Careers, marriage, kids, wills, RRSPs, mortgages, life insurance, disability insurance, inheritances, investments — what comes next? Well, do the words "empty nest" mean anything to you?

Don't panic, I am sure you are going to adjust. You are about to head into the stage of life when you have earned the right to do whatever you want to do, when you want to do it, and to do it your own way. So, get ready to take advantage of it. You could be starring in your own Freedom 55 commercial, jogging on that beach. It doesn't get any better than this, and that's why we call it Gold.

GOLD

FREE AT LAST

—

Gold is about attitude. Gold is not about age. Not everyone will experience Gold. Some people will not experience Gold because their life was limited by accident or illness. Some will not get there because they have no money. Others will not experience Gold because of workaholic habits that prevent them from getting out of Red until they land unceremoniously in Grey.

Gold was virtually unattainable a hundred years ago. Today it is readily available. Many factors are converging to make living a life in Gold the hot topic in the next two decades. One is that there is an increasing accumulation of wealth in RRSPs. Another is that in the next couple of decades, an unprecedented transfer of wealth in the form of inheritances will pass from those who lived through the Depression to their "live-for-today" offspring. Downsizing of large corporations and the public service is providing severance packages so people can make new choices.

The visibility of people in Gold will expand because of numbers and attitude. The numbers refer to the wave of baby boomers who are now in mid-life. This oversized cohort of people have upset the norms at every stage of their life. Their size alone has made them the focus of discussions and the media throughout their lives. They have created trends. Their attitudes have redefined what is acceptable and is encouraged at every stage of life. Their attitudes have been dominated by the worshipping of youth.

They were the group called teeny boppers. They created the hippies. They evolved into the yuppies. Now, they are going to become the Goldies.

Not every person born during the boomer years of 1947 to 1966 became a bopper, a hippie, or a yuppie. Not every boomer will become a Goldie. To become a Goldie will require an attitude that is focused on self-actualization. It will require an individual to seize control of his or her own life. It will require most people to reinvent themselves. Some will do so more than once during Gold. Above all, the standards by which they will make decisions will be their own. These standards will vary widely from person to person, and from year to year within each individual.

What could stop people from entering Gold? Well, lack of confidence in themselves; lack of courage to make changes; inability to state their own values, create their own vision, and take action; poor health that could be preventable through fitness; and lack of financial control of their lives because of debt and excessive spending.

Gold will not be a stage of life where people stop working. Some in Gold won't, some will. However, if they do choose to work, they will redefine their attitude to work. Work will have to provide them with much more than just money. The time dedicated to work will be on terms decided by the Goldie, not just the employer.

Golf has the Seniors Tour for professional golfers who have turned fifty. Lee Trevino has referred to this as a mulligan in life.

A mulligan is golfer slang for another chance. Gold allows everyone a chance to seize a mulligan in life. This time their game will be played by a set of rules they set for themselves. If they decide they do not like the rules, they will change them.

When I gave this book the title *The Gold Is in the Rainbow*, it was for two reasons. First, because Gold was in the middle of life, I thought it would act as a reminder that life is in the living. In my definition, Gold is a significant part of the journey and not some elusive, pot-of-gold destination at the end of the rainbow. The second reason was that I wanted to write something to help set an exciting path for myself and my peer group of early boomers as we prepare ourselves for that leap into Gold.

In the words of the poet Yeats, "We are happy when we are growing." Gold is about growing. Gold is about taking risks. Gold is about continuing to learn. Gold is about staying active.

The biggest difference between Red and Gold has to do with your attitude and your motives. Gold is the time when you rethink the social pressures that have fuelled your ambition. You free yourself from giving weight to "what other people will think." While your ambition may be lower, your need for self-actualization is higher. You accumulate fewer goods and are on a quest for experiences. Your attitude will be that growth through leisure activities is every bit as valuable as growth through work. Time focus changes from the future to now. You stop postponing. You come to an acceptance that you must live for the moment. You must act now. You accept the fact that "if it is going to be, it is up to me."

Ultimately, Gold is a gift you give yourself. It is the chance to have your life become what you always imagined it could be.

Throughout life, one of the greatest challenges comes from keeping things in balance. Gold is a stage of life that is not as clearly defined as the "go to school" environment of White or the more passive wisdom that will come in Grey. In Gold, the choices are endless.

Setting priorities will be important. We will still have competing goals from our career, family, personal health, leisure, personal learning, and our community. All these goals will compete for our time and our financial resources. Trying to keep them all in balance has always been important. In Gold they will have to be re-shuffled to create a new balance.

Many will now realize that the focus on work and career in Red may have left them with workaholic behaviours. In Red you may have served your job. If you are to become a Goldie, your job will have to serve you, or you may just dump the idea of having a job at all. Getting rid of these workaholic tendencies will require more effective delegation of work duties and a more focused use of your work time on accomplishing clearly defined objectives. Time for leisure will not only be more important, but it will likely become the status symbol to the boomer generation.

Making these adjustments will not be easy. It will take some time and effort to discover a new set of priorities for yourself. You will adjust most easily by setting attainable goals, appreciating what you do have, and being confident you can deal with problems as they arise.

WORK

Redefining yourself as being more than your job creates an entirely new personal vision. This can be a very liberating experience. Excitement rises when you do not put limits on what may be possible. Work can take on a new perspective when you change your motives. It can even become a liberator and a platform for personal growth.

Work will have been an integral part of your adult life. Work will have provided you with money, opportunities for growth, and access to many social contacts. Adjusting the role work plays in your life could mean some of these needs must be met differently.

Regardless of whether you choose to work full-time, part-time, or not at all, you will still have these three basic human needs:

- A need for routine
- A need for a sense of purpose
- A need for a sense of belonging

These needs have been most often filled through your occupation. Some of you have been raising children and you are consumed in supporting their daily routines. Gold is a time when you have to create new routines. In Gold a few may choose to put the same effort into grandparenting as they did into parenting. Some will choose scaled-down employment. Routines can be built around exercise programs, reading, hobbies, volunteering, or any other interest or activity in which you choose to involve yourself.

I can hear some of you expressing exasperation. "No way. I just got rid of my job and I do not want any commitments. Just leave me alone and let me do what I want, when I want." That strategy may be okay for a day off. It may even be enough to satisfy some people for a one-week vacation. But we are not talking about a vacation. This is the rest of your life. If you do not establish a routine you will drift. You will not accomplish your goals. You will increase your frustration and your stress. You will get bored. You will become boring. You will get old fast.

ESTABLISHING A ROUTINE

Knowing what to establish a routine around involves having a purpose. The purpose you choose is up to you and only you. Try using the same guidelines we set back in Green for choosing a career. Find something you are passionate about — helping others, a specific aspect of your former work, preserving the environment, travelling, yoga, or grandparenting. In fact it will likely be a combination of several of these. Some of them may seem totally eccentric. Who cares? A person who has many things about which they are passionate will always be able to create a routine that is dynamic. This dynamism requires changes. Your new routines will have to be flexible enough for some activities to be added and some to be dropped, either temporarily or for good. An inflexible routine is just a rut. Remember the old saying, "A rut is just a grave with the ends knocked out." Gold is about getting out of ruts, not into them.

With a purpose and a routine, you will not only learn and grow but you will be creating opportunities to be in touch with people. You will be part of a community. You will be living your life. You may still have time to watch and be entertained by a television soap opera, but at least you will not be living through them.

The biggest challenge you will face is identifying those things about which you can be passionate. Up to this point in their lives, too many people will have accepted the interests that others, or society in general, suggested. Not now. Not in Gold. This time it has to be your choices, because if you don't do it now, when will you? The answer is, you won't.

The people who were consumed by working in Red and did not develop other interests are not going to find this easy. A more gradual transition may be required of these people. New work structures are evolving. People are working part-time. They can now choose flextime. They may choose a temporary retirement to help prepare for full-time retirement. They may take a sabbatical. Many will choose to retire from one career and start a second career, which is similar to their old work but at a reduced level. Or the second career could be significantly different. One of the greatest opportunities is to become an entrepreneur. You could be a consultant or start a small business with low capital needs so that you do not have to bet the whole farm on its success.

I have four friends who all enjoyed great entrepreneurial success in their thirties and forties. Then they sold their businesses and retired. After two years, they had all bought new businesses. Two of them bought businesses in the same industry as they worked in before and two made complete changes. A typical comment from one of them could have applied to all four: "After two years of playing golf two hundred days and skiing forty-five, I was bored."

The good news is that they all recognized they were bored. All would admit that they failed to realize how important a role work had played in their lives. Their new businesses are important to them, but only one has become as immersed in work as he was before. I don't think he will ever retire again, and he may now work himself to death. The freedom turned out to be a frightening prospect. Do not feel sorry for him. He is very passionate about his new life. For him it took a temporary sabbatical to show him how much he really loved the game of business.

Now is no time to be timid. Now is a time to take a risk. I do not mean you have to risk all your money. I am talking about risking your image. Now is the time to run the risk of being a fool. Who cares if other people ridicule you? If they had passions of their own, they wouldn't have any time or interest in ridiculing yours. So find your own cliff to dive from and figure out how to swim when you are in the water.

Never allow yourself to commit that terrible sin of being a boring person. The only way to do it is to take some risks. You will know you are boring when:

- You get uptight every Sunday night, or worse, every morning about the prospect of going back to the job.
- You suffer from headaches and stress-related problems.
- You are staying at the job only for the pension.
- You don't have a feeling of control in your life and you are overworked.
- You don't enjoy the people you work with and they probably don't enjoy you either.
- You hardly ever talk to anyone about what you do. When you do talk about it, you even bore yourself. Fortunately, the people you are talking to just fall asleep.
- You are always complaining.

If you have some of these symptoms, it is time for some rear-view mirror thinking. Ask yourself this question: "When I am eighty and looking back, will I be proud to talk about what I accomplished by doing this job for the next ten years?" If the answer is a firm no, then quit, and get on with it.

I spent twenty years with one company. I had different positions during that time, but my most recent position had lasted fourteen years. In the beginning I loved the job and the life it allowed me to lead. But I reached a plateau. I felt that when I was eighty and looking back it would not make any difference if I was in this job fourteen years or if I stayed for twenty-eight years. However, the excitement of reinventing myself was wonderful. I quit. I became reinvigorated by my career. I now know that during the next fourteen years I will have some interesting stories to talk about when I am eighty.

Does this mean transition is easy? No. In my case I had to give up a twenty-year career, relocate, create a whole new network, re-establish my credibility, re-establish a social life, and because it involved starting a new business, I had to do all that without an income.

Most people concluded that I was either crazy or had a lot of guts. They also figured I must have a great wife who was willing to go along with all that change. They were right on all counts.

Was my transition easy? No. Was I alive? Absolutely. Will I talk about this adventure when I am eighty? You bet. Do I recommend that you follow your own dream? Emphatically yes. Otherwise you are doomed to a life of quiet desperation, living your life with those "cold and timid souls that know neither victory or defeat."

Now, in my case things have turned out okay. I can still remember some of my thoughts and emotions leading up to the decision. Although I was very apprehensive about the outcome, I knew that I would not be true to myself if I didn't move on. It also helped to put things in perspective. In a hundred years, no one would care. As a matter of fact, almost no one cared at the time. It was my life and I just had to live it.

My advice to you: Come on in, the water is fine (shiver, shiver). Will it be easy for you? No. Nothing easy ever makes much of a difference. Will it be successful? Likely not in the beginning. You will likely look the fool for a while. Just remember, no one else cares. When they look at you struggling they will just be glad it's not them. Then when you succeed, they will say you were lucky.

As treacherous as this road appears, I believe it is about to get very busy. My boomer cohorts are at that time of life when not very many of them will have caught the brass ring in big corporations or in civil service jobs. I think that once the financial responsibility to their children eases, they are going to be jumping out of these jobs in droves. They are going to seek a redefined version of the adventurous lifestyle they experienced in their youth. Out with hippies, in with Goldies.

This is good news and bad news for employers. The good news is they were planning on pushing a lot of people out anyway. The bad news is, the ones they were hoping to keep are the ones who are going to jump first.

In financial matters, these Goldies will have a pleasant surprise. Once they follow their heart and do things they are passionate about, they will find the financial rewards more than adequate. Remember what we talked about back in Green and Red? Wealth comes to those people who find something they like to do and keep doing it for a long time. The same rules apply in Gold.

Ultimately, your occupational security comes from your own abilities and talents. Have confidence in them and give them every opportunity to flourish. When you are eighty, you will be proud of yourself and so will your grandchildren. You sure wouldn't want to be giving these grandchildren a speech about following their own dreams if you didn't follow your own. When they ask you, "Did you follow your dreams, Grandpa/Grandma?" you'll be able to answer that question with confidence and an exciting story or two.

Following your dreams will prevent your becoming boring to the rest of the world today. The excitement and confidence you feel inside will allow you to be one of those people who can be both interested and interesting.

Some people are going to choose to keep working at the same career. However, they will make changes in how they do their job. They will make changes in their attitude to the work. Their need for power will decline. The joy in mastering their craft and sharing that craft with others will become paramount.

It is this sharing with others that opens up the greatest opportunities for people. It can be called mentoring, or focusing on a life of significance, in which what you do for others is more important than what you do for yourself. You become a true helper of others.

"It is better to give than to receive": This is one of those lessons preached to us early in life. Until now we may not have figured out how to fully incorporate it into our working lives. Gold is the time to do it. You will have to give up some of your own ego needs. People development will be your focus. You will need the patience to let them fly with you until they can fly alone. You will have to train them, protect them, encourage and motivate them. Then you need the confidence to let them go. It requires confidence to train your successors and your future supervisors. When you have completed this process with one person, start on the next protégé. This process of helping other people to grow is one of the most satisfying that you can experience in your life. It also helps create the most enjoyable and motivating work environment for yourself and those around you.

LEISURE

As people progress in Gold they will gradually focus less on work and more on leisure. While some may find that they never retire, others will retire as early as possible. Some may retire more than once. Along this process, people will have opportunities to learn how to live without work providing the central part of their routine.

Baby, this can be wonderful. The limits on how wonderful are only in your own imagination. You can do things you never had the time for. Things you only had a little time for may become central. Use some thought and imagination to help plan and create some exciting options. Leisure can give you a routine and purpose by helping others, create opportunities to learn and grow, and provide you with social contacts. These are the things you need to have a joyful and active life. Now no one is putting limits on you. Unfortunately, you do have to get up off your butt, turn off the television, and get out there and make it happen. Hopefully you will have incorporated some leisure activities into your life while you were working. These activities will reduce stress, enhance your life, and likely prolong the period you will want to keep working.

When you commit to new leisure activities, you will experience a period of discouragement and frustration. You will be the new kid on the block. Everyone else seems to know people and know what to do, only you are the rookie. Just sign up. Do something, anything. Very soon you will start to re-establish confidence and contacts. Remember how tough it is for you to get restarted. Then you will be the first to reach out with a helping hand for the next new arrivals.

Most organizations need more people and will be thrilled to see your interest. One of the best things you can do for these organizations is recruit a friend and get them involved too. Be careful — if you recruit too many people, they may recognize your leadership skills and put you in charge. Maybe that wouldn't be so bad. So push yourself a little at the start of each new venture and the doors will quickly open to activity, personal growth, and friendships.

Here are some quick suggestions.

- Join a service club like Rotary or Lions. They have meetings, people, and built-in committees and projects that need help. Many of these service clubs are eager to accept women.
- Travel with a purpose. Go see something specific that you are interested in. It could be a wine harvest in Portugal, a photographic safari in Africa, seeing a Formula 1 Grand

Prix race in Europe, or a Shakespearean play in England.

- Go to Quebec City and enroll in French immersion.
- Join CESO (Canadian Executive Services Overseas) and volunteer to go on a one-to-three-month project to help a business in another country. A friend of mine has been on over twenty of these all around the world. There is no better way to travel inexpensively, help other people, and be hosted and learn all at the same time.
- Take a canoe trip in a provincial park. Sea kayaking is another great option.
- Go fishing. Stop just hanging up the sign saying you are gone, and actually go.
- Your fitness program may now be a daily social event and not just something you have to squeeze into a half-hour. Join the "Y." Get involved in exercise classes. Use their other programs. Do not limit yourself to the things you did when you didn't have the time. Fitness is a necessity. The use-it-or-lose-it theory certainly applies. The need for activity increases after age forty-five. Just do it.
- Golf is the perfect game. It takes a long time. It is in a beautiful place. You get exercise, and you are with people. So what if your score isn't so good? The best golfer is the one having the most fun.
- Old timers' hockey. Apparently these guys don't know when they should quit. So join them.
- There are many other sporting activities, such as curling and lawn bowling, that you may never have tried. Why not now?
- Playing bridge is an activity you can virtually do forever and there are many clubs and groups you can join.
- Bird watching is one of the most popular activities these days. Most communities have groups you can join on hikes

to share the experience and get information. This is also a great focus for a trip to some new place.

- Gardening is also incredibly popular. Don't just stick a plant in the ground. Learn about them. Exchange cuttings with neighbours. Offer to help out doing the garden for a neighbour with six kids and a full-time job. They will appreciate the help and will likely pay you a little too.

- Volunteer at your local hospital or art gallery. This gives you a chance to help others and meet lots of people.

- Learn about your local library. Dollar for dollar this is the best value in town. There are no limits on what you can learn. Volunteer to help them too.

- Be the world's best grandparent. If you do not have grand-kids, become a Big Brother/Sister or help out with Boy Scouts, minor sports, or Sunday school.

- Sign up for education classes. They can be at night or you might just go back to university or college full-time. Who says you can't? You might want to skip the Thursday night pub crawl, though.

- Attend church, join the choir, or get on the church board. Every organization needs good people. Your church is no exception.

- Join a political campaign and help a candidate or a cause.

- Seek out opportunities to help others, like Meals on Wheels.

- Take up ballroom dancing. You can do it with a spouse or friend, or you can go alone — you may meet someone who becomes a friend.

- Go for a walk every day. This is also very beneficial to your health. You may be surprised who wants to join you. However, as with all your other activities, you must be prepared to go alone. You cannot sit back and wait for others. Nothing may ever happen.

- Read the newspaper every day. It provides an activity and keeps you involved and current with the world.
- The most important thing of all is to allow time to do nothing. Learn how to limit your activities so that you can enjoy them in a more quiet and unhurried way.

You have all heard the numbers. People are living longer. Women on average are living past eighty and men are close behind. This means you may be talking about a lot of years from an early retirement in your fifties. Make use of this time. Boomers have always been the high priests of our youth-oriented culture. They are going to redefine aging and do everything in their power to grow old youthfully. I am hoping to shoot my age at golf. If I meet this goal, an awful lot will have gone right in my life.

HEALTH

I have made several comments about using your fitness program to provide activity to your life. Do not forget about the benefits to your health. We are not talking about everyone running marathons. All you need is moderate exercise to maximize the benefits to your health. I stress moderate — exercising to peak performance can often lead to injury.

Without your health, many of your other plans will come to naught. Keep active. Some people may find that a major health problem, like a heart attack, may be just the wake-up call they need to get some priorities rearranged in order to allow them to move into Gold. Sometimes what seems like the worst news may be the warning you needed.

Here is something you must do: Get a physical regularly, every two years at the very least. Women need to be on the alert for breast cancer; with men it's prostate cancer. All of us run risks on many other health issues. Early detection is an important factor in deciding about treatment and in its success. If you think you are too busy for this, let me suggest a psychiatrist as well as a physical.

WHAT, WHO, WHERE?

Back in Green we talked about these three key questions: What do I want to do? Who do I want to be with? Where do I want to be? In Gold you still have to answer all three questions. So far we have focused on what you want to do. However, who we are with is a central part of our lives. Statistics suggest that men in particular benefit from having a spouse or close companion. Those who enjoy long and stable marriages not only have companionship but a lifetime of shared memories and relationships.

As we age, many adjustments occur in our relationships. Kids grow up and we are left with an empty nest. Friends retire and move away. The most difficult adjustments deal with losing a spouse through divorce or death. Do not be embarrassed to seek professional help to deal with these adjustments. However, you will come to realize that you still have a life to lead. If you get active, opportunities for companionship will develop. This does not have to mean romance or marriage. Romance is just like everything else in Gold. You are in charge. You make your own rules.

Seek out organizations that cater to middle-aged and senior-aged single people. They can provide excellent opportunities to meet people who share your need for companionship. A widow friend of ours met someone at her first meeting. They have now vacationed together and have been great companions.

Where you live may have been dictated by your career. Gold creates opportunities to rethink where you want to live. Prior to making these changes, give some consideration to how far you are willing to move from friends and family. I said *some* consideration, because while you may not be keen on moving away from them, they may just up and move away from you. In the end, you have to accept that you will be building new friendships and relationships throughout your life regardless of where you live.

Here are some of the interesting options that are popular today:

- Move from a big city to a small town. Usually this decreases your cost of living, and the lifestyle is less hurried. Personal security is often cited as an advantage. Communities like Elliott Lake, Powell River, and Cornwallis have all made an effort to attract people who have retired. These communities provide low-cost housing and recreation. Many towns provide full access to health care. For those who want to keep working, these towns offer fewer opportunities, unless you are self-employed and your business can move with you.

- Move from a house to a condominium or an apartment. Usually the cost is much lower than a house. Even in a market where housing is very expensive, like downtown Vancouver, there can be other cost advantages. You may need only one car or can just rent one on weekends.

- Move to areas in which you have enjoyed your recreation in the past. Places like Whistler, the Laurentians, Collingwood, and Niagara-on-the-Lake are all popular.

- Move closer to your grandchildren. For some people they will become the main focus of their life. Make sure this move is welcomed by your kids and their spouses before you do it.

- Move to a university town and re-involve yourself in education or just enjoy the environment in these communities. Kingston and Antigonish may be worth considering.

- Climate is often a big motivator in people choosing a community. As we age we become more susceptible to the cold. This is a scientific fact, not a rationalization. Vancouver Island will continue to attract increasing numbers of people, especially as out-of-country health costs become prohibitive in the future.

- Health costs be damned, a lot of people are still going to want to be snowbirds and migrate each winter to places in Florida, Arizona, California, and Texas. Before making a large real estate investment in any area, try visiting the community for a vacation several times. Cost of accommodation in these areas can vary from extremely expensive to almost embarrassingly inexpensive in some manufactured home communities. Some people insist they can live more cheaply for the six months in the south than they can at home. These people may choose to make the summer cottage their Canadian home and get rid of the bigger house in the city.

- Sunbelt areas have many communities that are set up exclusively for seniors. A few of these communities are starting to show up in Canada. Some people love the activities, the security, and the companionship. Others may find a community that focuses on only one age group somewhat isolating.

- Get a good RV and you can set up a new home wherever you choose. You can stay forever or keep moving with the wind.

- Why limit yourself to the United States? Try Mexico or Costa Rica. The climate is great and the cost of living low. These are not developed countries, though, so you will encounter significant adjustments in the way of life. Remember, the main language is not English or French.

- Some people pack up and move completely to destinations where the main motivation is to pay fewer taxes. Cayman Islands is one of the best known. If this is a permanent move for tax avoidance reasons, get good advice from a professional in advance. Many restrictions apply to what you can do or own in Canada. It may sound like utopia but the drawbacks should be assessed first.

Lifestyle is up to you. Don't just accept what you have today without considering the options. You may be surprised how invigorating a new environment can be. If you choose an attractive community, you may find the kids and grandkids visit more often and stay longer, even though you are farther away. Don't get caught up in worrying about the risks — choices can be changed. Frankly, they can be changed more than once. Some of the Goldies who own an RV or are travellers will be changing them all the time. Freedom was the common theme of the hippies and it may return for some Goldies, but on a different scale. Who knows, maybe psychedelic VW vans will make a comeback.

MONEY

It is time to address the financial matters for Goldies. In the beginning, I said not everyone will become a Goldie. Some may not make it for health reasons, some because of a workaholic focus keeping them locked in Red. But most people will prevent themselves from entering Gold because of the poor management of their own financial affairs.

Does it take a lot of money to be in Gold? Not necessarily.

How much money is needed can vary greatly depending on the choices made by the individual. If you are happy to choose a lifestyle that requires very limited resources, then Gold can be attained easily. If you want a champagne lifestyle that will be indexed to inflation, you'd better make a bag full of money in Green and Red and save a lot of it, because you will be needing it.

This may seem a dumb and obvious question. Can money make you happy? No. Does having money mean you will be unhappy? Of course not. Happiness has more to do with attitude than money. However, having enough money to support the lifestyle of your choice will affect your attitude. A positive attitude is enhanced when you feel you are in control of your financial affairs. Your lack of debt and your retirement planning mean no one else can pull your strings. Not a banker, not an employer. It is a statistical fact that life expectancy is affected by your income. The National Forum on Health reports that health is affected by your ability to have control over the decisions in your life. Increased wealth gives you more choices, and hence, a greater sense of being in control.

You can make a quick assessment of how much financial control you have now by considering the following scenario. Your boss fired you today. Could you adjust to the new circumstances with full confidence that you and your family were going to be okay? Would you be at the mercy of the bank or other lenders? What could you do to prevent them from calling your loans, scooping most of your savings, and foreclosing on your house?

When you have set up your affairs so that an event, like losing your job, can be dealt with and no major disruptions occur, then you are financially ready for Gold. You may still have to rebuild your confidence and your attitude but that is entirely in your control.

Naturally, those people who place very little value on material goods have an advantage. Their lives are not being run by the "stuff." They are in charge to choose when they want to move into Gold. Does this mean everyone with money will be in

Gold? Unfortunately, no. A lousy attitude, an inability to set up a routine, a lack of purpose, no non-work-related interests, or poor health can also prevent a person from living a life in Gold. We have talked about these issues already; now let's focus on the financial priorities.

DEBT

Number one, as always, is debt. Some business debt may be necessary. In these cases the interest costs are deductible from income for tax purposes. But even in business, no debt is better. It will be difficult to be in Gold if you have not eliminated debts on which interest expense is non-deductible. One possible exception would be on money borrowed to invest in an RRSP. In these situations it is normally best to borrow only what you can pay back in one year. Otherwise the non-deductibility of interest becomes self-defeating. It is still much better if you are fully contributed to your RRSP and you are making your annual contribution in advance.

Mortgages should either be paid off or reduced to the point where the cost of carrying the debt is significantly below the cost of renting. You may want to rethink whether leasing a car is such a good deal. You would be surprised how much you may enjoy driving a five-year-old car on which there are no payments.

The worst kind of debt to still have is credit card debt. Frankly, if you are taking on any debt for lifestyle reasons, you had better go back and read some of the things we talked about in Purple, Green, and Red. Remember, you simply cannot spend more than you make and be in control of your own financial affairs or your life. And you certainly cannot enter Gold.

So what can the debt-burdened person do as he or she approaches Gold? Accept the fact that the jig is up. You are going to have to adjust your lifestyle. If you do not, circumstances will catch up with you anyway. Then you will have to deal with these matters on someone else's terms and the impact will be greater. You will be vulnerable if you are forced to retire early. Downsizing may result in unemployment at a point in life where getting a new position at the same income level is very difficult. Health issues may also force you to make changes that affect your income.

Here is what can happen when you hit the wall financially:

- You lose your income, employment insurance is slow in coming, and it provides you with substantially less income.
- The bank calls and takes away the line of credit and the credit cards. Not only that, they want you to pay up what you owe. Now. They can force the liquidation of assets or even bankruptcy if you do not make your required payments.
- If you have debts with Revenue Canada, you are really asking for trouble. These people mean business. They will not show any sympathy, nor should they, with the difficulty you face in reducing your extravagant lifestyle.
- The lender forecloses on your mortgage as soon as you miss a payment or two and they learn that your sources of income are gone.
- Your leased car gets taken away. If you own the car but it is assigned as collateral, it still goes.
- Your RRSP may get scooped to cover debts. This would not apply to a company pension plan. It also may not apply to an RRSP set up with a life insurance company. These pension moneys can have creditor protection under the law. If you have your RRSP with the same bank that gave you the loans, they will be quick to seize these assets to cover the debt.
- Your life insurance and disability insurance lapse.

Enough gory details. I think you get the picture. If these things happen when you are twenty-two, they are bad, but you have time to rebuild and change your habits. If you are over fifty, it is much worse. You may not have the time or be given the opportunity to recover. You are also dealing with bad habits that have been actively cultivated for over thirty years. These spending habits will be hard to change. Basically you will have condemned yourself to a life of hand-to-mouth survival on government support. This is not Gold. This is not your being in control. When you become dependent, even if it is for financial reasons, you skip directly to Grey. Most people would prefer to wait many years until Mother Nature takes them to Grey. Nobody wants to get there early because of poor financial planning.

If you are financially vulnerable, it is time to take action. Otherwise, you will never have the freedom or the confidence to do the things you want with your work. You will always be too desperate for every dollar of income. You will be operating from weakness, and you will have transferred the control of your life to other people. The fact that you are unhappy with this situation will not help. It is only going to get worse unless you make changes.

Yes, you have to make the changes yourself before someone makes them for you. Now may seem late, but it beats all the alternatives. Here are some suggestions you can take now:

- Cut up all your credit cards. If you do not have the cash for something, don't buy it.
- Do an item-by-item expense summary and identify areas where you are overspending. The boat and the golf club membership may have to go. Restaurants and takeout food are out, eating at home is in. This is just the beginning.

- Have a garage sale and get rid of all the junk in your life. You will be shocked at how much there is and how much money can be made. Make sure any money raised goes to pay off debts.
- Re-assess your automobile costs. If you have a lease, can you get out of it without huge penalties? Can you get by on one less car?
- Re-assess your housing costs. Can you downsize? Move close enough to work that you can walk? Is renting an option? This could free up equity in your home to pay off debts and get caught up on your RRSP. Can you move to a less expensive community?
- If your spouse is not working, he or she might have to get a job.

This is going to be a slash-and-burn exercise in order to regain control of your life. It may be painful at first but the freedom can be quite exhilarating. When you begin to see the light at the end of the tunnel, you can decide whether you want to continue working or not. You can start to enjoy your leisure, instead of worrying about the next payment. And you can feel confident that you can be happy and comfortable in how you choose to structure your retirement. These are benefits you likely never imagined for yourself as you rushed through life chanting your theme song, "I owe, I owe, it's off to work I go." As soon as you start forgetting the words to this song, you begin preparing for Gold. The debts will be gone, including the mortgage. Cash freed up by downsizing can start producing an investment income.

Now, before you go hog wild and choose your new theme song as "Take This Job and Shove It," think about your long-term financial needs. Yes, you may now be able to change your attitude to your present work. You may restructure it to meet your needs, which may include working flextime, using your vacation time, taking a sabbatical, or changing to part-time work. If given a chance to experience a trial retirement, many people find they actually want to keep working. The key is that you will now be doing it on your terms.

One-third of all early retirees choose to return to work and this trend is growing, according to Statistics Canada. The majority of these people take part-time positions. The reasons for returning to the workforce were varied but included the need for money, personal preference, and the need to have something to occupy their time.

INFLATION AND BENEFITS

There are two cruel realities that many early retirees forget about. The first is inflation. The second is the constant lowering of government benefits for the elderly.

Do a quick calculation about the impact of inflation by using our old reliable Rule of 72. If inflation is 4%, then every eighteen years the cost of everything will double. A fifty-five-year-old may find it difficult living on the same income at age eighty. The buying power of the same money may be only one-third of what it was when he or she retired. Women should pay particular attention to inflation. Living longer than men has rewards, but it leaves women more vulnerable to the consequences of inflation.

Being a boomer has had advantages and disadvantages. One big disadvantage is that the system — any system — has been swamped. When we were in school, portables were erected to deal with increased numbers of students and more schools were built. When we got out of school, the disproportionate number of job seekers to jobs available was known as youth unemployment. When we were in our twenties and thirties, the cost of residential real estate skyrocketed just when we wanted to buy.

Now that we are getting ready to retire, is the system any better prepared to deal with us? Today, there are five people working for every one being supported on universal government pension programs. In thirty years, when we swamp the system, there will be only three people working for every one who has to get his or her nose in the trough. The government will not have the money, so there will be fewer old age pension benefits and not everyone will qualify for them. Universality will be gone. There will almost assuredly be an increase in the qualifying age for government benefits from sixty-five up to age sixty-eight or higher.

If you are nervous about your government pension, wait until you see the impact the boomers will have on health care. On average, over 70% of all a person's medical costs take place in the last six months of his or her life. With the boomers swamping the health system, the government will want to download more health costs to the individual.

What should you do? Don't just sit there. You had better be preparing your own retirement plans. You had better expect to pick up more of your own health costs in retirement than your parents are paying today. And the cost of health insurance when travelling outside Canada is going to escalate dramatically.

So before you jump into early retirement, sit down with your financial adviser and crunch the numbers. You may be disappointed that you have to keep working a little longer than you thought. However, it is better to find out now than wait until you are seventy-four and find you are behind the old eight ball financially. This will not be the time to be sending out your résumé. However, all the statistics suggest that many boomers will be having to do just that. It is expected that the boomers will become a new generation of impoverished seniors as their high-spending days catch up with them. Only a small percentage of people will be rolling around in their golf carts in the sunshine.

EARLY RETIREMENT

Early retirement is subject to the triple whammy. First, if you retire early, you have fewer years to contribute to your pension plan or your RRSP. Second, there are fewer years for compounding interest to work in your favour before you start stripping out the growth to live on. Remember, working eight more years allows your nest egg, invested at 9%, to double, even if you do not contribute any more. And third, you need this money to pay you an income for a longer period of time. After all, if you end up living to eighty, the money has to last only fifteen years if you retire at sixty-five. If you jump out of the earning game at fifty-five, the money has to last twenty-five years.

In the good old days the majority of people had company pension plans. Today more and more people are required to look after themselves through an RRSP. If you are self-disciplined and invest the money wisely, a personal RRSP is an advantage. If you do not make contributions or if you invest the money poorly, you are going to become one of the increasing numbers of working seniors. That may not be bad if the work you get is enjoyable for you. However, not everyone will be so lucky. Most will be doing it because they need the money. Finding work you enjoy seems to happen only if you don't need the money and you are in a position to negotiate the terms.

Even though you may have retired from your initial career by choosing a second career, it can help you avoid two of the three problems in the triple whammy. First, if you can earn an income you may not have to draw on your pension, so its compounding growth continues. Then, when you stop this second career, you have more money to spread over fewer years. The third whammy, inflation, just keeps marching on. In this scenario, if your debts are paid and you have a retirement nest egg built up that is growing, you may need only to meet your expenses. Your savings and debt may be looked after, so your income needs can be quite a bit lower.

TAXES

Just because you are in Gold does not give you any sanctuary from taxation. They still want your money. You still need to stay on top of things to make sure the government gets no more than that to which it is entitled. If your second career is one of self-employment or your own business, many opportunities exist that can benefit your personal tax situation. Many tax planning books are available at your local bookstore. A good tax adviser should always be able to more than offset the cost of his or her advice with savings in taxes. The same is true in the longer term with the advisers you have for your estate planning.

ESTATE PLANNING

A proper will is essential to make sure your estate is settled according to your wishes. Check out what we discussed in Red. Probate fees, which can be reduced with planning, have been increased lately. In Ontario they are 1.5% of your estate and in British Columbia they are 1.4%. Only Quebec has resisted the temptation to make this tax grab.

The same advisers should help you set up a power of attorney in case you become unable to manage your own affairs. This can be done relatively easily when you are healthy. If you become incapacitated without having completed a power of attorney document, your family will be required to make application to the courts to get things done. This costs money and takes a long time. Just get it done at the same time as you are getting a will.

INSURANCE

Once your will and powers of attorney are done, keep them up to date. This is especially important if you divorce, your spouse dies, or any person you have selected to act experiences changes that might make it more difficult for him or her to fulfill the responsibilities.

It may be too late for some people to get more life insurance. If you have been adequately covered until now, you may have some choices to make. If you have permanent insurance, you may be in a position to stop paying premiums and still maintain the coverage. You may also be in a position to make additional contributions to these contracts where the growth in their value is sheltered from tax. A permanent insurance contract is an excellent method of preparing to pay funeral costs or taxes due on death. Such a policy prevents other assets from being sold to meet these obligations.

If you have term insurance, your annual premium costs will be getting higher. You should sit down with your adviser and assess your short- and longer-term needs for life insurance. Now would be a good time to convert a portion of your term coverage to permanent insurance, so any long-term needs can be met. This conversion is almost always a guaranteed option with term insurance you own personally. If you have only group insurance, you may be out of luck unless you still have your health and are insurable. If you still do not have a financial adviser, get one.

Disability insurance becomes prohibitively expensive at later ages. If you have done an adequate job of maintaining proper coverage through Red, you will not likely need to buy any more, just keep what you have already. For those making the jump from the big company to a second career, you may need to obtain some disability coverage because your group coverage will cease.

Your Retirement Expenses

Use this worksheet to determine your annual living costs.
You'll see that some expenses will fall in retirement, while
others will rise. List all figures in today's dollars.

	Today	When You Retire		Today	When You Retire
Home			**Personal**		
Mortgage/Rent			Health club		
Property taxes			Grooming		
Renovation			Clothing		
Maintenance/repairs			Dry cleaning/laundry		
Heating			Other		
Electricity			**Leisure**		
Water			Vacations		
Cable TV			Telephone		
Furniture			Theatre/Film		
Housekeeper			Books		
Other			Newsletters		
Food			Memberships		
Groceries			Education		
Meals outside of home			Other		
Liquor			**Insurance Costs**		
Tobacco			Health insurance		
Other			Life insurance		
Health			Disability insurance		
Medical (not covered by insurance)			Home insurance		
Prescription drugs			Other		
Non-prescription drugs			**Loans**		
Dental costs			Car loan		
Glasses			Personal loans		
Other			Line of credit		
Transportation			Other		
Auto purchase			**Retirement Savings**		
Leasing payments			RRSP contributions		
Gas			**Miscellaneous**		
Auto insurance			Alimony payments		
Auto licences			Child support payments		
Parking			Gifts (Christmas, birthdays, etc.)		
Public transportation			Charitable donations		
Other			Pets		
			Total Current Expenses		
			Total Retirement Expenses		

Your Retirement Income

	Annual Income
Company Benefits	
Defined benefit pension plan	_____
Money contribution plan (estimate)	_____
Government Benefits	
Canada Pension Plan	_____
Quebec Pension Plan	_____
Old Age Security or Seniors Benefit	_____
Registered Investments	
RRIF income	_____
Annuity income	_____
LIF income	_____
Non-tax-sheltered Investments	
Stocks	_____
Bonds	_____
GICs	_____
Mutual funds	_____
Income property	_____
Other	_____
Income from Home Equity	
Income generated by selling your home	_____
Income generated by reverse mortgage	_____
Business & Employment Income	
Income from job	_____
Income from business ownership	_____
Total Income Expected at Retirement (before tax)	
Less estimated annual taxes	_____
Total Income Expected at Retirement (after tax)	

You can likely get your own group plan even if you only employ yourself. Your retirement funds may offset some of your need for disability protection. Assess your personal needs with your adviser.

Financial Planning

So much for the basics. Now let's get on to planning how you can live for today. The first piece of advice never changes: Keep your expenses low. Buying things for the sake of buying things is no more gratifying in Gold than it was in Green or Red. Keep the "stuff" to a minimum in your life. Overconsumption may seem to be good for the economy but it is not good for you.

Financial planning takes a different twist when you start spending your savings. The focus changes from constantly putting money into your pension plans. Here are some of the questions your financial planner should be helping you to answer:

- How much money do I have?
- What are my lifestyle and financial objectives?
- When can I retire?
- What can I do to help protect myself from inflation?
- What other estate issues should I be planning?
- What tax planning can I do?

You will need more than one adviser. Usually you will need a lawyer, a tax adviser, an insurance adviser, and an investment adviser. You will pay up front for legal and accounting advice, but usually insurance and investment advisers are compensated on commission.

Every year, draw up a net worth statement. Simply add up what you own, then subtract what you owe. This gives you your net worth. Then do a projection of your expenses for the next year.

Your financial planner will have access to computer software on which he or she can enter your assets, liabilities, your retirement objectives, your projected investment returns, your expense forecasts, and your expectations for inflation in the future. The program can quickly calculate how much more you need to contribute or how soon you can retire on what you already have saved. This is a very useful exercise. The computer programs rely on assumptions about investment returns and inflation, so no answer can be considered final. Things will always change. The key thing is to update this analysis regularly and make the necessary adjustments to all the factors. Constantly refining the information will allow you to get closer to your ultimate objectives.

The income of most retired people comes from their company pension plan or their RRSP. Those who've had a long career and a company pension plan should be able to get their projected retirement income at various ages from their employer. Knowing these numbers will help you answer these key questions:

- When can I afford to retire? How much other savings will I need to supplement my pension from work?
- How much does my earned income exceed the pension income I could get now? Is it worth it to keep working? Could I go part-time? Could I quit and get a second career of my choice?

Many long-time employees are offered incentive packages from their employers to retire early. They should not just jump at the offer, but do the math and make sure the benefits outweigh the fact that they will be losing their job. If you are one of these people and you enjoy what you are doing, it may not be worth it. However, many people will find this a catalyst to move on to Gold. If the package is as a result of downsizing or termination, consider getting legal advice before accepting it. Wrongful dismissal suits are quite common and employers must meet established expectations.

LUMP SUMS

A severance package or a retirement allowance may come as a lump sum. If they do, you have some options available to you that could save you a great deal on income taxes.

This is definitely a time to sit down with your financial adviser and discuss your options. First, you will need to prepare to cover your living costs. A money market account should serve you well in the short term by providing interest income but leaving your options open. You may need to access your money, or you may wish, at some point, to invest it long-term. Once you have been re-employed or have set your retirement plan, a longer-term investment strategy can be set. Be careful of the tax year end. If you do not make decisions by then, you could lose some options and pay a heavy tax burden.

You can use this lump sum to make your annual RRSP contribution or to make retroactive contributions to your RRSP. The amount of additional money you can contribute is contained in the Notice of Assessment you get each year acknowledging that your tax return has been reviewed and accepted. You might make contributions to your spouse's RRSP. Spreading the contributions between your spouse and yourself can give you more equal incomes in retirement and thus provide some tax benefits.

Additional contributions may be made under the retiring allowance formula. The formula allows that for each calendar year you were employed up to 1996, you can contribute $2,000 per year to your RRSP as a retiring allowance. If this is a direct transfer from your employer, no withholding tax will be withdrawn. This "rollover" provision has been eliminated for years after 1996. However, for the years prior to 1989 that you worked for this employer, you can contribute an additional $1,500 to your RRSP for each year you were employed where you did not have a company pension plan, or that your employer's contribution to your pension plan or Deferred Profit Sharing Plan had not vested at the time of your retiring allowance.

Any additional severance payments in excess of this formula will be classified as income and taxed in the year received. You could benefit if you can convince your employer to pay out the money over two years, especially if you do not become re-employed quickly.

If your financial situation forces you to take money out of your RRSP at this time, remember that any withdrawals are subject to an immediate withholding tax. The actual tax you owe will be established when you prepare your tax return and could exceed the amount already withheld. My advice is not to touch your RRSP unless your house is being repossessed or the food bank is your only option. Remember, this is your tomorrow money, and tomorrow has a nasty habit of coming sooner than you think.

RRSPs

RRSPs are at the centre of most people's financial plans. If you have not been able to make contributions, start doing so right away. Making the maximum payments to your RRSP is the ideal strategy. Try to do it every year and as early in the year as possible. Set up a monthly contribution with an employer or through a mutual fund company so you are consistent at putting in the money. If you borrow to contribute to your RRSP, do not spend the tax saving on lifestyle. Use it to reduce the debt. Make sure the loan is repaid in one year. Otherwise, you will not be in a position to make next year's contribution but will be further in debt. As well, the interest paid on an RRSP loan is not deductible, so the exercise becomes self-defeating.

If you are behind on your RRSP contributions and a financial windfall or inheritance allows the opportunity to make a catch-up, by all means do it. Your tax adviser should be consulted to prevent problems with the minimum tax rules, which can be imposing.

Now that you have all this money in your RRSP, what should you do with it? I suggest you use the same investment strategies discussed in Red. The eight-cylinder approach provides diversification of your investments. A few of these investment cylinders should be in equities, which have traditionally provided the higher return over time. Your equity investments should focus on different countries, investment styles, and different managers. You should always try to have the maximum 20% in foreign content. Growth in equities is an excellent way to offset the effects of inflation on your retirement planning.

Other cylinders will focus on non-equity investments like bonds, mortgages, and real estate. These may be a little less volatile than stocks but their return over time has generally been lower. Some money may be placed in risk-free investments like GICs. No matter how risk-free a bond, mortgage, or GIC appears, they are still only as good as the people, company, or assets behind them. The CDIC (Canada Deposit Insurance Corp.) insures up to $60,000 on a GIC at a bank or trust company. Bonds from the federal or provincial governments are backed by their ability to tax, which is as close to a sure bet as you get. Corporate bonds usually provide a higher return than government bonds, but you would be wise to use a mutual fund to get the necessary diversification and professional management.

Mortgage mutual funds can be more risky than a GIC, but a

well-managed mortgage mutual fund will provide excellent diversification and higher returns. There are also mutual funds that own real estate or stocks in real estate companies. The latter has more liquidity.

Recalling the birthday cake theory of funds discussed in Red, put together a program for yourself that provides security in the cake. The icing is made up of investments that have a little extra risk but help provide some additional growth. And to satisfy that bit of greed you may have, add a candle fund or two. With a little luck you can brag about their performance — and the wild ride they are sure to take you on.

As you approach retirement, your tolerance for risk will change. Your investment adviser will work with you to help set your comfort levels and help you sort through all the investment options. Through ongoing reviews, you are kept on target to reach your goals, with a level of risk that prevents you from losing any sleep. After all, if you can reach your goal without risk, why would you take any?

OUTSIDE YOUR RRSP

Some investments and assets will not be in your RRSP. Most people will have a home. Gold may provide the opportunity to move to a smaller home, thus eliminating debt and potentially freeing up some capital. This money could be used to make those RRSP catch-ups or to make some non-registered investments. Some of you may choose to put the money into winter accommodation in a warm climate.

LIVING IN THE UNITED STATES

Make sure you work closely with your tax adviser if you are planning on spending more than an average of 120 days per year in the United States. This average is calculated by taking half of the days spent in the U.S. in the current year, one-third from the previous year, and one-sixth from two years previous. If you plan to spend this much time in the United States, you will be considered a non-resident alien and have to complete forms for U.S. tax purposes. If you receive U.S. rental income, you will also have to complete tax forms. Canada has a tax treaty with the United States, so although you are not likely to owe tax, you will still have to file a U.S. tax return. However, as your U.S.-generated income increases, you may be required to pay taxes in the United States. If you have substantial assets there, you may ultimately become vulnerable to their high estate taxes. Many books have been written on these topics, and Douglas Grey's *The Canadian Snowbird Guide* is a very good one. Make sure you discuss your tax position with your adviser if you are planning to spend lengthy periods in the United States.

Recreational Property

Some people choose to invest in recreational property. Potential capital gains liabilities can be created when the property is sold or deemed to be sold at your death. Only your principal residence is excluded from capital gains tax. If your intention is to keep this property in the family, you will have to do some planning, which should include the kids and your advisers. Emotional issues often are connected with a cottage more than any other asset. Address these now. Otherwise, you may have planted the seed for future discord among your kids.

Selling Your Business

For some people, their largest asset will be their business or their farm. Plan carefully to maximize the value of your investment and minimize income taxes that could be triggered at disposition. You must involve your advisers in these discussions.

Do not wait until the last minute. In order to qualify for the $500,000 tax-free capital gain on the sale of a small business corporation, you must have been incorporated for two years and have had over 90% of the assets active in the business. This requirement eliminates holding companies or other businesses that have been used to shelter significant investment income in the corporation.

You will recall that we talked about buying a business back in Red. Well, now the shoe is on the other foot. Now *you* are the one who wants to cash out. Figuring out an exit strategy is often overlooked by business owners caught up in the day-to-day running of their business.

Potential buyers will be looking at a few key things. Above all, they will be looking for profit. If there is no profit, your business may have very little value. Other key items will be cash flow, growth, a market niche, and employees with the skills to carry on the business.

Next, you will have to identify potential buyers. One of your children may be interested. Another potential buyer could be a key employee or a group of employees. How are they going to get the money to pay you? Usually, you will have to take back the financing if selling to family members or employees. Are you prepared to do that? You may have to stay involved in the business for a while in order to protect your investment. The earlier these transition plans can be implemented the better. The business maintains direction and the key employees now take on the commitment of owners.

A large competitor or a public company may also be interested in buying and may not have to ask you for financing. However, they may want you to take part of the payment in the form of shares in their company instead of cash. And they will likely want you to stick around for a while.

In each case, you do not get a cheque and quickly disappear. That is why planning in advance is so important. Get a plan in place. Like most planning, the details may change over time. You may be handling more money in your exit from the business than any other transaction in the business's history.

NON-REGISTERED INVESTMENTS

In Red we discussed how all of your non-registered investments are not taxed the same. Interest income is taxed the same as earned income but cannot be used in calculating RRSP contribution limits. Rental income is considered earned income and is eligible for RRSP contributions. It also allows deductions from gross income for expenses and from net income for depreciation on buildings. Only 75% of capital gains are taxed. Capital gains that can be deferred are not taxed until they are realized. Dividends on Canadian corporations are taxed at the lowest rate.

Keep these tax issues clear when assessing the benefits of an investment. It's not just the rate of return that counts. The important figure is what you keep after the taxman has taken what may seem like a disproportionate share.

Give serious consideration in Gold to the time and expertise required to make good investments and manage them. Mutual funds are popular not just because they have produced good, tax-effective returns. They also require very little management or expertise on behalf of the investor. They provide a great variety of investments and all of the accounting and tax reporting for you. If you have firm ideas about how you want to spend your time in Gold, do not get stuck managing your investments. Give them to the professionals to manage and go play, unless you regard watching the TSE index bounce around as a spectator sport.

PENSIONS

If you keep your health, you will still be in Gold when you are able to qualify for the Canada Pension Plan and the government-supported pensions. Although the contributions for CPP are going to increase significantly, the plan will be there as a source of income for most Canadians. That level of income is modest at $736 per month for a sixty-five-year-old who qualifies for the maximum, which many people will not. Contributing to the CPP is mandatory, and the contribution rates are increasing to 9.9% by 2003. Remember, the CPP does have many desirable features from a public policy perspective: all working Canadians qualify; it is vested to them immediately; it is portable from job to job; it is fully indexed; and it has special benefits for disability and at death. One of its biggest positives is the low administrative costs of 1.3%.

If you are no longer working, you can qualify for CPP as early as age sixty. Your benefit is reduced half a percent for each month before your sixty-fifth birthday. You also can delay collecting until age seventy. In this case, the opposite happens, and you get an extra half a percent for each month you delay beyond age sixty-five.

Old Age Security (OAS) is the other government-sponsored pension program. It provides an income for people over sixty-five who have lived in Canada over ten years. However, don't get your hopes up. Everyone gets it, but not everyone gets to keep it. The amount a person receives is subject to a clawback for those with net income over $53,215. For every dollar of income over this level, 15% of the OAS is clawed back, until it is all gone when your income exceeds $85,528. Keep this information in mind if you were over sixty on December 31, 1995.

The final part of the government pension program is the Guaranteed Income Supplement (GIS). This is not a universal program. Only lower-income seniors qualify. For a single senior with no other income, the maximum from OAS and GIS is $10,264 per year. For a couple, it is $16,642 per year. These figures are slightly below the statistical level of poverty in Canada, according to the National Council on Welfare.

For low-income Canadians, the government programs may be their entire income. The level of these incomes allows many low-income people to more than replace the 70% of their pre-retirement income. As pre-retirement income increases, the individual will need to be more involved with providing the desired retirement income.

It is difficult to plan for your future around government benefits. The government is desperate to lower its future costs. Until now, the whole system has been supported by favourable demographics: lots of baby boomers working, with relatively few seniors. This will change in the next couple of decades when we have lots of baby boomers retired and the baby bust generation left to pick up the bill. Governments have enjoyed taking the political credit for helping today's seniors. However, they do not want to support the boomers as they age, so get ready for lots of political fights and misleading rhetoric. The federal government already tried to replace the OAS and the GIS with a Seniors Benefit that would have reduced their long-term cost. The Seniors Benefit was repealed in 1998 after the government received a lot of political pressure from seniors and boomers. However, there is a built-in benefit reducer in both the OAS and the GIS because they are not fully indexed to inflation. The clawback levels are also not adjusted for inflation. This can make a big difference in your income after a few years. No matter what, all seniors in the future are going to get less from the government. Many boomers of average and above-average income will get nothing. If you happen to be born in the baby bust generation and are doing a little reading ahead, your situation is the worst. Start saving now: your parents and grandparents may just leave the cupboard bare.

Do not expect the age of eligibility for government pensions to remain at sixty-five. University of Waterloo professor Robert Brown presents the case for its rising to sixty-eight or higher in his thesis, "Economic Security for an Aging Canadian Population." The United States has already announced the age of eligibility will go up to sixty-seven in 2026. What a coincidence! Just when the peak of the baby boom reaches retirement age, they change the qualification age for benefits. Do you think your Canadian government won't do the same thing?

COMPANY PENSIONS

How you take income from a pension plan at work will depend on the type of plan it is. If it is a defined benefit plan, you will receive a guaranteed retirement income. The amount you receive will be based on a formula tied to your level of earnings and the length of time you have worked. Be careful if you are a high-income earner (i.e., your income exceeds $86,111 per year). The maximum income the government permits these plans to provide is $1,722.22 per year of employment to a total of $60,278 per year. If you have high earnings, you had better do some additional planning and not rely exclusively on the company plan.

In order to control their future costs, more companies are choosing to implement pension plans in the form of a defined contribution plan, sometimes called a money purchase plan. Your income will depend on how much money you and your employer have put into the plan and how effectively it has been invested. This is similar to your RRSP. What your eventual income will be is more difficult to predict. It will be affected by your age, the amount of money in your plan, interest rates, and the guarantees you seek on the pension income.

Many people do not have a company pension plan at all. They must rely on what they have saved themselves in their RRSP. Others will have a combination of a company pension and personal RRSPs.

USING YOUR MONEY

Hopefully, you have maximized the money available for your retirement. Now in retirement you want to take the money out. Even if you do not need the money, the government says you have to start taking it out of your pension plan or RRSP by the end of the year in which you turn sixty-nine. You can take the money out of your RRSP in one of several ways. The most popular is a Registered Retirement Income Fund (RRIF). Other options include an annuity, cash, or a Life Income Fund (LIF).

The RRIF gives you the most flexibility. Here are some points to remember about a RRIF:

- You are required to take out a minimum percentage from your RRIF each year after age sixty-nine. You can take it out earlier if you wish.
- The annual percentage that must be withdrawn increases as you grow older (see table).
- Income from a RRIF can be paid out annually, quarterly, monthly, or as an extra lump sum where allowed by the trustee handling the money.
- This income can be deposited directly into your bank account.
- In the year you set up your RRIF, you are not required to withdraw a minimum amount.
- Taxes are not withheld by the trustee on minimum payments. Income taxes are withheld on payments that exceed the minimum.

How to Calculate the Minimum Amount of a RRIF

Age at January 1	Minimum Withdrawal %	Age at January 1	Minimum Withdrawal %
65	4.00	80	8.75
66	4.17	81	8.99
67	4.35	82	9.27
68	4.55	83	9.58
69	4.76	84	9.93
70	5.00	85	10.33
71	7.38	86	10.79
72	7.48	87	11.33
73	7.59	88	11.96
74	7.71	89	12.71
75	7.85	90	13.62
76	7.99	91	14.73
77	8.15	92	16.12
78	8.33	93	17.92
79	8.53	94+	20.00

Note: The first withdrawal takes place in the year following the year the plan is set up. The above percentages are based on the RRIF value on January 1 of the year the withdrawals are made.

Withholding Tax		
	Quebec	All Other Provinces
Up to $5,000	21%	10%
$5,000–$15,000	30%	20%
Over $15,000	35%	30%

Note: The withholding tax applies to amounts of RRIF withdrawal above the minimum amount.

- You may change your RRIF plan trustee at any time. The existing trustee will make the minimum payment for the year to you.
- The minimum payments can be reduced if you base them on the age of a younger spouse.
- Any spousal RRSP that you contributed to will commence based on your spouse's age and not yours.

- At the time of your death, the proceeds of a RRIF will roll over tax-free to your spouse if he or she is named as the beneficiary. This designation can be in the RRIF contract or in your will. If your spouse is not the beneficiary, the money becomes taxable to your estate.
- You can convert your RRIF to an annuity in the future. But once you have chosen an annuity, you cannot go back.
- Normally, it is easiest to combine your RRSPs into one consolidated RRIF.
- You can keep all the same investments you had in your RRSP or change them if you wish. Diversification is always recommended. Remember, you could be retired a long time so do not lose a growth focus in your investments. However, most people will become more risk averse as they age.

The second option is an annuity. This is a much more predictable option and may be desirable to the conservative investor. Here are some points to consider about annuities:

- Term-certain annuities are an option that provides a fixed income until age ninety. They are available through banks. They are unpopular and are not recommended because you might outlive your money.
- Life annuities provide a guaranteed income for the rest of your life. Life annuities are only available from life insurance companies.
- Investment risk is eliminated with an annuity. The life insurance company providing the annuity takes all the investment risk. However, they keep any benefit of superior investment results.
- The mortality part of an annuity is a calculation about

how long each person will live. You choose a number of years you wish to have the payments guaranteed, even if you die. Most people choose ten to fifteen years, which at least guarantees the return of their original capital. After this guarantee period, no other money will be paid to your estate on your death. However, it will pay you an income as long as you live. The shorter the guarantee period, the higher the income. This may be fine for someone with no close heirs and good health.

• Many people choose a joint annuity with their spouse. The income continues until the death of both spouses.

• You can negotiate an income that starts out lower but is adjusted to inflation.

• You can have both a life annuity and a RRIF. The RRIF helps offset inflation and gives you an opportunity to choose some growth investments. The annuity gives you the guarantees.

• You can buy an annuity from a RRIF. You may consider this as you age and no longer want the responsibility for investment decisions inherent in a RRIF.

• Annuities are much more attractive when interest rates are high.

The third option for your RRSP money is a cash withdrawal. This is not usually recommended because you have to pay tax on the entire amount, which is added to your income in the year of withdrawal. Some taxes will be withdrawn at source before you get the money, but more could be owing when you do your tax return for that year.

The final option for your RRSP money is considered a hybrid. It applies only to people who left an employer with a pension plan, rolled the money out of the pension plan, and were

required to put it into a locked-in RRSP or a Locked-In
Retirement Account (LIRA). These cannot be turned into cash.
Locked-in accounts must convert to a life annuity or a Life
Income Fund (LIF).

LIFs are similar to RRIFs. However, there are some differences:

- There is an age requirement before you can withdraw an
  income. The minimum age varies by province.
- There is a maximum percentage you can withdraw in a
  year.
- You are not allowed to base your level of withdrawals on
  your spouse's age.
- The biggest difference between a LIF and a RRIF is that
  you are required to convert your LIF to an annuity by the
  time you reach eighty. If you are married, this has to be a
  joint-and-last-survivor annuity with your spouse. In some
  provinces, an LRIF is available instead of a LIF and it
  does not require you convert to an annuity.
- LIF rules vary from province to province so talk to your
  financial adviser.

How you combine all your government, employer, and personal pension options will depend on your situation. Gold will
likely be the most critical time in your life to be talking to your
financial adviser. All your decisions could involve large amounts
of money, and some of these decisions are irreversible. Once you
have looked at all the issues that you are forced to deal with by
government legislation, re-examine how you can best use any
non-registered investments you have.

Some of you will be so well off that you may just kiss the
OAS benefit good-bye and not worry about it. Some will be at
an income level below where the clawbacks start. In the future,

many people will find that managing their income to minimize the clawback will be a key part of planning. So your priorities will vary depending on your situation. This includes splitting income with a spouse. Everyone will be trying to pay as little tax as possible and yet still have the income they need to support their lifestyle.

One of the keys to being able to live on an income below the clawback level is to have no debt. Your home, your car, your recreational or winter property, your RV or other toys, should all be clear of debt. Your costs for them are then limited to maintenance, utilities, taxes, and insurance. You will need a lot more income if you have to pay rent and lease a car. Naturally, all the other methods of keeping your expenses low still apply.

OTHER SOURCES OF CASH

There are some areas beyond just your liquid investments in stocks, bonds, mutual funds, and savings accounts that may be useful sources of cash. This money may be accessed in a way to help your lifestyle and not appear as income, which can free up more money to spend without putting you offside on the clawback. These options include refinancing your home or rental property, liquidating a life insurance policy, and other options that don't involve lump-sum payments.

Your Home

One place to find this money is in your home. If you were to sell and downsize, it would free up cash. If you simply refinanced your home, it would generate a lump sum of tax-free dollars. Unfortunately, it would also generate a monthly mortgage payment. This is an option you may consider for the short term until you do sell your home or repay the mortgage with an inheritance or the sale of a cottage or other asset.

A reverse mortgage is a more formal way of getting income from your home. It provides you with an income at the same time as you continue to live in your home. This sounds like having your cake and eating it too, but it does create a debt obligation against the home, so your equity value is being reduced. However, much of the income is considered a return of your capital and is not taxed. This is a strategy I believe will become more popular in the future. However, it is not well suited to early retirees. The income will be small and the debt obligation will become large as you age.

The same strategy of refinancing a rental property would create tax-free dollars. In this case, the mortgage would be covered by the rent and the interest would be deductible. If you sold the rental property, you could realize a capital gain on which taxes would be owing, so refinancing may be a better option than selling.

Life Insurance
A life insurance policy with cash values can also provide cash. If you just take out the money, most of the cash will be fully taxable as income. However, if you use the policy as collateral, you can get the cash tax-free. The debt can ultimately be paid off with the proceeds of the policy. With very careful planning and documentation, you may even have the interest become tax-deductible if the money has been used for an investment.

Several of these suggestions are ideas that trigger a lump sum of money, but many people prefer a regular income that is also tax effective. There are a couple of options for putting that lump sum to work other than just putting the money in a GIC, getting only the interest income, and having it fully taxed.

PRESCRIBED ANNUITIES

A prescribed annuity is a very conservative option for dealing with a lump sum of money. It differs from a life annuity because it has a set period of time, usually five or ten years. You deposit the cash and receive a regular monthly cheque. At the end of the period, all the capital will have been returned to you plus interest, and there will be nothing left. The majority of the monthly cheque you receive will be a return of your capital, which is not taxable. The other part of the monthly income is interest income, which is taxable. You can choose to have the amount of annual interest income equalized every year rather than being higher in the early years and lower towards the end.

SYSTEMATIC WITHDRAWAL PLANS

The second option is to place the money in a mutual fund and choose to receive a systematic withdrawal from the plan each month or year. The fund itself will hopefully continue to grow and you would be subject to the normal taxes. The systematic withdrawal will result in some income taxes being paid on the growth, but a portion of your monthly income is considered capital and is not taxed. Most of the growth will be capital gains and is taxed at a lower level. The percentage that is capital gains will vary with the investment style and the performance of the fund.

Many people who receive a large sum of money from the sale of a business or a property may use a prescribed annuity for five years to guarantee them the income they need and put the remainder of the capital in a mutual fund. This allows time for the mutual fund to grow, and their income is not affected by the short-term fluctuations in the market. It also defers taxes on the growth of the mutual fund. After the annuity runs out, you simply repeat the process with a portion of the capital in the fund.

Psychologically, these tools are very good. Most people in

retirement want a predictable source of income. Talk over some of these options with your financial adviser. Spending capital can be emotionally difficult. When you have spent a lifetime building your nest egg, it is sometimes satisfying simply to sit on it. In my family, my father finds it easier to spend his money when I remind him of what I will do with it if he doesn't. What do you think your heirs are going to do with your money?

Remember, it is just money. It is not security. Your only real security is who you are and the people you love. However, money can help in gaining experiences. Just because you are getting a little further along in the game, there is still room for some rear-view mirror thinking.

REAR-VIEW MIRROR THINKING

Ask yourself, when I am in Grey, what do I want to say I accomplished in Gold? You cannot put a price tag on memories, so go and get the memories that are important to you. It may be later than you think. Now is not the time to procrastinate.

Gold sounds awfully good. You have freedom. You have money. You have control of your life. Why would anyone want to leave? Mother Nature has her own set of rules. Nothing lasts forever, so it is farewell to Gold. But with a little bit of luck, you will spend some very satisfying years in Silver.

SILVER
CONTENTMENT

—

Life is a process: each stage contains opportunities to learn and discover things about ourselves. In each stage, you set different priorities and ideally found each stage to be interesting and enjoyable.

Silver can appear at first to be a retreat from Gold. In some ways, it is. In other ways, it is a choice to stay a little closer to home and discover things about ourselves that we may have overlooked or underdeveloped as we got caught up in the "hurry" of the other stages.

When a colt is born it starts in the barn, then moves to the corral, next to its mother. Then it is on its own to learn about everything the ranch has to offer. In time it will be ready and willing to come back to the corral. This return to the corral is Silver.

There are many reasons and motivations to return to the corral. The most obvious is your own health. Over time we can experience many breakdowns in our health. The most common problems of aging include arthritis, high blood pressure, osteoporosis, diabetes, and obesity. Unfortunately, the list can become much longer. Many of these can be deferred or minimized through exercise and diet. However, deferred does not mean eliminated. It's the same old story: you can run but you can't hide.

Another reason that often brings people back to the corral is the health of a spouse or a significant other. In these cases, your focus becomes that of a caregiver. Focusing on the needs of another can be very gratifying, but it can also be very demanding.

Financial resources may also limit you to the corral. You have a lack of money to do the things you want. The costs of education, transportation, entertainment, and recreation can be prohibitive. You can make less expensive choices, but they may seem a poor compromise compared to activities you once enjoyed.

Attitude has been a big part of all that you have done up till now in your life. It is a big part of what Silver can become. A poor attitude pushes people prematurely into Grey. Remember, you control your attitude. No matter the circumstances you face in life, you are the one who has the power to interpret them. You may be surprised at the opportunities that can be found in adversity. You also know people who have been able to find dissatisfaction with every situation, no matter how good it looked to others.

For those with an optimistic attitude, Silver provides an opportunity for growth. For those who are pessimistic or prepared to surrender and give up, Silver is just another stage of that slide into the abyss. The good news is that their defeatist attitude will reduce the time they get to spend in Silver. The bad news is that their poor attitude will prevent them from enjoying anything in Grey. So what is the hurry? None of us are going to get out of this alive.

Silver is at its best when you focus on the opportunities it provides. Minimizing your potential is easy. Just choose to do nothing, be a grouch, lose your friends and don't make any new ones, get fat, become self-centred, be bored and boring, all at the same time. As your grandkids would say, "Get a life." Maybe it's time you listened to them.

Silver is the time of life for reflection. It is the time when the pieces of the puzzle that are your life have all come into focus. When I've talked about using rear-view mirror planning, I meant that you were looking back from Silver. Now you are here and you are entitled to look back and enjoy the view of the things accomplished. You are also able to put failures or things unattained into perspective: Nobody won all the time, but are you proud of how you played the game?

RELATIONSHIPS

Silver may also provide the opportunity to right some wrongs in your relationships. Take the opportunity to gain understanding with your own children. It will be satisfying for both of you. Perhaps a little forgiveness of yourself and others will be needed.

Above all, Silver can provide the opportunity to observe, love, enjoy, care for, pamper, spoil, and brag about your grandchildren. If you do not have grandchildren, adopt some. Many a kid out there would love to have all the things a grandparent can provide. You just love them and let them be the centre of the universe. You may never know how deeply you have touched their lives. But there will be no doubt how they can touch yours.

MYTHS OF OLD AGE

Perceptions of old age are in the eye of the beholder. Frankly, there are many myths. It's true that most people do have some health-related issues but the vast majority feel well most of the time. Unfortunately, many become victims of poor lifestyle. The chickens come home to roost for those who have had no exercise and have maintained poor nutritional habits.

Another myth is that older people lose intelligence. There is no evidence to that effect. As long as a person has an active mind there is no rapid drop in intelligence as we age, perhaps only a slight reduction in short-term memory, which is more of an inconvenience than anything else. There is no evidence that you get any brighter, either! So just because you get more opinionated is no reason for people to pay more attention to those opinions.

Older people are frequently portrayed as unattractive and sexless. This, too, is a myth. Any observer will see just as much flirting at a senior centre dance as at a high school dance. In fact, interest in sex and romantic relationships goes on forever.

One other myth is that older people are all the same. In fact, they are just as different now as they have always been. The personality of a person does not change with age. It actually becomes more pronounced, for better or worse. If you have been a jerk all your life, pity those people who will have contact with you when you are in Silver, because you are going to be an increasingly bigger jerk.

One thing that is not a myth is that people who are older are subject to discrimination and prejudice. There is a great denial of age in our youth-focused society, which leads to a stereotyping of the aged. Let this be a warning for those of you in Silver. It is a mistake to let others decide how you are to be judged. For some this stereotyping will become a self-fulfilling prophecy. We need a vibrant vision of aging, and today's seniors can be the pioneers in creating this new vision.

GAINING PERSPECTIVE

When the boomers were young, they came up with self-serving catch phrases like "never trust anyone over thirty." They have now lived long enough to see the error of their ways. They now want to see age defined in a way that will be more attractive to them. They are looking to today's seniors to provide leadership and help create that new image.

What is the reality beyond the myths? The fact is that when you get older, you will not feel any different. If you feel well, and most older people do, the choice is to be active, to act young. Most older people feel themselves to be the same person they were when they were young.

Their needs in Silver are mostly the same as they were throughout their lives. They want a safe environment. They want friends and plenty of activities to share with them. They want to feel encouraged and supported by those around them.

However, the dominant need throughout our lives has been for a sense of purpose. That is still required. Nobody can give it to you. You have to make a sense of purpose for yourself. Losing it leads to loneliness, fear, and uncertainty, resulting in brooding, boredom, and an altered role in your community, all of which will accelerate the aging process.

The first thing you need to do is get an attitude — a positive attitude! Attitude comes from within. Your attitude has to be one that assumes you will continue to grow. This path of growth is your purpose. People do not grow old, they just run out of purpose. Or, as a wise man once said, "You don't grow old by getting old. You get old by not growing." Developing this kind of an attitude requires optimism. It requires a positive self-image. It requires an openness to take pleasure from the daily activities of your life.

So what are we seeking? What is the most meaningful thing you can live for? Ultimately, it is to reach our full potential. When you look at your life you may ask yourself: "Is my life's work done?" The answer is simple: "If you are alive, it isn't."

Reaching your potential may require you to do more of what you have done in your life up till now. It may require you to make changes and reinvent yourself, forcing the learning of new skills and the development of other talents. Either way, it is always more fun splashing away in the water in an attempt to master swimming than it is sitting passively as a spectator at the side of the pool.

FINDING YOUR WAY

Choosing your purpose in Silver will involve making the same basic decision that was required in Purple, Green, Red, and Gold. Find something about which you can be passionate, something that you can lose yourself in, something that you feel is bigger than you are, so that when you are doing it, time passes quickly. Then do it.

Let me make a couple of biased suggestions. Do not expect or search out any external approval for what it is you choose to involve yourself in. If it comes, fine. Maybe by this point in your life, you will have learned how to similarly treat what Kipling called "the two impostors of victory and defeat."

The second biased suggestion is to become nonjudgmental of the choices of others. In Silver you should now have the understanding that each person is facing his or her own challenges and could use encouragement. At the risk of being accused of encouraging physical abuse, let me say that sometimes a well-placed kick in the butt can be the ultimate act of friendship. If you choose to administer this treatment, always offer a helping hand to the person who has to make the adjustments. Starting a new journey or taking a new direction is never easy.

WORK

In Silver when I refer to work, I am referring to your life's work and not employment. Traditionally, people in Silver no longer have paid employment, although this is changing. Two factors are contributing to this change. The first is the reduction in government pensions, so seniors need the extra money. The second is a change in attitudes towards hiring of seniors. Wal-Mart is a very visible example of an employer broadening its attitudes. Many of their door greeters are seniors. McDonald's led the way with a commercial of a senior's first day on the job. However, if you really want a glimpse of the future, visit any town in southern Florida where you will find jobs in restaurants, grocery stores, and shops predominantly filled by seniors. I had my groceries bagged by an eighty-five-year-old the last time I was there. The airport shuttle van was being driven by a seventy-one-year-old widower who said he retired eight years ago. I asked how often he worked and he said five days a week. He still thinks of himself as retired. Go figure.

Frankly, in Florida and Arizona, there are more jobs than there are young people to fill them. When the baby boomers hit Silver, and the baby busters are in Red, that will be the case in Canada as well.

FIGHTING LONELINESS

The biggest fear among seniors is loneliness. This becomes most acute for widows and widowers. Widowers have a much higher chance of remarrying, with the result that much of the loneliness of old age is a female problem — widows outnumber widowers by about five to one.

The main source of life's energy is interaction with people. We yearn for friendship, conversation, and mental stimulation. The need for contact with other humans does not diminish with age. However, where school and work easily guaranteed this contact, it may now be more difficult to develop. In Silver you cannot just sit back and wait for people to find you. You have got to get out there and find people with whom you can share life's experiences. Just because you decide to relocate to a community in a warm climate does not mean you will not be lonely. It takes more effort to make friends in a new environment.

For the fortunate, families play a large role in providing the needed contact. However, people in Silver would be unwise to overuse these relationships. Your kids have very busy lives. Cat Stevens's old song "The Cat's in the Cradle" reminds us how when we were in Red, we were sometimes too busy for our kids. Now that we are in Silver and they are in Red, they are often too busy for us.

In order to keep these relationships with your children positive, try not to dominate, try not to give unsolicited advice, and try not to criticize their lifestyles. Do not complain too much about your health problems. Try to solve as many of your own problems as you can, and retain as many of your own friends and interests as you can.

It also helps if you and your adult children can deal with each other as equals. You have to teach your kids how you want to be treated. They will often be struggling to understand your expectations of them.

The typical family setting is not always an option for single seniors. Some may not have families or they may be separated from their families by long distances. But a blood relationship is not a prerequisite for a relationship between people. Seniors can choose to live with other people. The television show "Golden Girls" was based on just such a situation. Seniors can provide help and service to others, whether that be volunteering to help with Meals on Wheels or babysitting for a single mother. Senior centres are focal points for activities. The opportunities for contact with people are limited only by your imagination and your willingness to go out and make something happen.

Remember, if you are lonely, so are a whole bunch of other people in Silver. It is the same story as the high school dance, with boys on the one side and girls on the other. Somebody has got to take the first step so you can both end up with what you want. Resolve to make yourself the person willing to take the first step. Just say hello, introduce yourself, and start a conversation. Some of these conversations may last only a moment, some will lead to friendship. Taking this initiative will not only be good for you, but many other people will be very grateful you did.

Those fortunate enough to have friends and a sense of community find that these relationships take on greater importance. They have now ceased to be ambition-bound and can focus more on people and the simple things life has to offer. At this stage in their lives, they can focus on the reality and not the image. Loyalty and companionship are the two most highly valued qualities. In Silver you know yourself, and can now be more at peace with yourself. You are coming to terms with the meaning of life.

Statistically, it is unlikely that a couple can stay married for a very long time and both live long enough to reach Silver together. When it does happen, this relationship can be very deep. Communication takes place without a word being spoken.

Unfortunately, nothing lasts forever. Widowhood is extremely common in Silver. The grief felt about the loss of a lifetime companion can be overwhelming. This grieving process involves feelings of isolation, sorrow, and, of course, dramatic change. A source of strength, support, and companionship is gone. It creates a vacuum that you think can never be filled again.

GRIEF

We are not taught how to deal with grief. We are uncomfortable and awkward in talking about it. The grieving process is portrayed as a story with a beginning, a middle, and an end.

In the beginning, we are in shock and are surrounded by

friends and family. After about a month despair sets in and supportive people are not around. A sense of loneliness and resentment exists. Well-meaning friends offer platitudes like "I understand how you feel." You feel isolated. Grief never completely ends, but in time it will reduce in intensity. Here are some suggestions psychologists have for dealing with grief:

- Accept the turmoil.
- Allow the necessary time to adjust to your new circumstances. Go slow.
- Tell your own support people what you need.
- Speak openly and often with others.
- Expect upsets on anniversaries.
- Focus on your health. Take walks. Get plenty of rest. Laugh often.
- Distract yourself with work, reading, and hobbies.
- Pamper yourself. Be gentle with yourself.
- Don't fight the fear. Go where you fear to go.
- Do something for someone else.

Friendships based on couple-centred activities are often disrupted. Many widows left the handling of the money to their husbands. Now comes added responsibilities and challenges. Some widows even took much of their public identity from their husbands. Widowers may now be doing things in the household that were previously done by their wife. Often only others who have experienced the same level of loss can understand and console. However, over time both widows and widowers make varying degrees of adjustment to the reality that life goes on.

HOUSING

Many times in Silver we change accommodations, either willingly or unwillingly. Leaving a family home may not be desired or recommended because of memories and friends. Unfortunately, physical problems and financial pressures often make a change necessary. The success of any move will depend primarily on the attitude of the individual involved. A positive attitude towards the change will happen only if the person involved has made the decision. Often, family and friends may become overly involved. The person in Silver must continue to make his or her own decisions, which may not always be popular with everyone, but they should be respected.

The type of new housing can vary widely. Some options are private homes, condominiums, apartments, retirement communities, and senior citizen homes. Your choice must provide you with a feeling of comfort and security. The proximity to activities, friends, a neighbourhood, and needed services should all be considered. Privacy is also a factor sought by people in Silver.

Some people in Silver may relocate to a new community to be closer to family or to live in a warmer climate. However, people often forget how important their old community and network of relationships were to their well-being. A warm climate with no friends is not a home. A new city where your kids are busy all the time with their own lives is not necessarily what you bargained for. Normally, only those who are very independent, who can adapt easily to a totally new situation, and who can make friends easily should consider such a major move. Even they should do it only after visiting and spending time in the new community. If you are lonely now, a move is unlikely to make a difference and may actually make things worse.

HEALTH

Now that you have made it to Silver, you may think you no longer have to exercise — that's for young athletic types. Wrong!

What you do not use you will lose. Lack of fitness will cause your muscles to lose strength, your skeleton to become fragile, your heart and vascular system to become more vulnerable, all of which leads to obesity, depression, and premature aging. This is not a pretty picture, but it can be counterbalanced by involving yourself in activities that you find enjoyable. Your fitness routine should focus on building strength, flexibility, and endurance. You will find your mental attitude improves. All this will lead to an increased life expectancy and far greater personal satisfaction.

Hopefully this commitment to exercise has been lifelong. It was a poor trade-off if you sacrificed your health for your career. But even if you plead guilty to this offence, it is never too late to start exercising. Exercise helps increase the enjoyment of your life. It may be a thirty-minute walk or an exercise class at the "Y." If you can't motivate yourself, get a dog. It will stand at the door staring at you so that you won't be able to resist an outing. A pet provides many positive psychological benefits as well.

Part of being healthy includes good nutrition. The old rules still apply. Eat a balanced diet, consume very little fat, restrict red meat, drink skim milk, and consider some vitamin and iron supplements. Of course you should not smoke, and alcohol should be consumed only in moderation. A person in Silver may require only 60% of the calorie intake of someone in Red. As always, moderation is the best policy. You should plan your diet and exercise in consultation with your physician.

EMOTIONAL HEALTH

The final part of your well-being is keeping yourself fit mentally. Just because you are in Silver does not mean you can't learn new things. That may be true for old dogs but not people. Keep informed on current events. Learn a new hobby. Fantastic educational programs are available to seniors through organizations like Elderhostel, senior citizen centres, community colleges, the "Y," and churches.

MONEY

You are not done with financial matters either, though there are changes in your financial priorities in Silver. Earning an income is no longer the big issue. Using your assets to provide an income, planning your estate, updating your will, and considering charitable gifts become more of a focus.

You will have some fixed income each year from your pension plans with the government, your company, and your RRSP. The RRSP income may be in the form of a life annuity or a RRIF. Prepare a budget every year to make sure your income from these sources will cover your expenses. If shortfalls exist, other assets may be available to provide additional income. If the annual revenues do not exceed your expenses, you will be consuming capital. Your financial planner can work with you to set up a plan so the money doesn't run out before you do.

We talked in Gold about financial products like prescribed annuities, systematic withdrawal programs from mutual funds, and the possibility of using the capital in your home in the form of a reverse mortgage, as ways to supplement income. Then there is that other great financial planning tool — spending less. Wasting your money is not any smarter in Silver than it was in Green.

Once you have your income and expense needs figured out, you can move on to the topics that take on more urgency in Silver:

- Do your heirs know where to find all your important documents? This includes your will, tax returns, investment accounts, ownership papers, insurance policies, and birth and marriage certificates. Have you prepared a personal inventory of your assets? Do they know where your safety deposit box and key are located? Do they know the names and addresses of your advisers?
- Make sure you have a will. Review it and bring it up to date. Divorces, remarriages, deaths, and new births may need to be taken into account. Have you named a backup executor?
- Review any life insurance policies. Who is the named beneficiary? If it is your estate, the money will be subject to probate fees.
- Do you have up-to-date named beneficiaries on your RRSPs, RRIFs, LIFs, pension plans, or DPSPs (Deferred Profit Sharing)? If your spouse is the beneficiary, these assets can be rolled over to him or her, tax free. Otherwise, the money becomes taxable to the estate.
- Have you or your accountant estimated any taxes due on your death? Where will the capital come from to pay these taxes? This would include capital gains tax, probate fees, and taxes on RRSP money. If you have assets in the United States, you may have to pay estate taxes there.
- Have you prepared instructions for your funeral? Have you prepaid or set money aside for your funeral? The cost will likely exceed $5,000, so it is a significant expense. Funerals seem to cost much more if decisions have to be made by family members at a time of high emotional stress, your death. The money to pay for it could come from investments or life insurance. The best solution is to prepay the costs with a funeral home.

- Have you set up a power of attorney? This will give legal power to a person or persons to act on your behalf regarding financial assets if you become incapable of doing it yourself. Without a power of attorney, the courts will assign someone to look after your affairs after you become incapacitated. This is a time-consuming process.

- You may also want to have a separate power of attorney apply to decisions concerning health care measures you will receive. Some people prefer not to have extraordinary medical effort taken just to prolong their life. You are putting your loved ones in a tough spot if you have not communicated your wishes and given them the authority to make sure they are carried out.

- Consider holding ownership in real estate such as a home or cottage in joint tenancy. This will allow the asset to pass directly to the joint tenant without its being listed for probate. Get legal and accounting advice so that no unexpected taxes are triggered on your death and you understand the ramifications about control of the property.

- If you own a business, is your succession plan in place? Make sure you explain your plans to your whole family and not just those who will be inheriting the business. For larger businesses, the key employees should be informed about what will happen to the company. After all, it's their livelihood as well. There are many tax issues you should be discussing now — while you are in reasonably good health — with your financial adviser, your accountant, and your lawyer.

YOUR ESTATE

Simplifying your estate is one of the most useful things you can do for yourself and your heirs. I recommend Sandra Foster's book *You Can't Take It With You* if you have an estate of any size at all. Plan your estate so that you pay the government fewer taxes and minimize internal family strife in the future. Abdicating your responsibilities will be appreciated only by the government and the legal profession. I doubt if you feel either of these is a worthy charity for your hard-earned money.

Most banks, investment advisers, and trust companies can provide you with a free booklet to help you summarize all the information your heirs will need. It is unbelievably helpful if all this information is in one place and they know where it is.

One of my biggest hopes in writing this book is that it will help initiate more intergenerational discussions about money matters. Too often your adult children do not know what your financial situation really is. They do not know if they should expect an inheritance. They will need to understand how your estate will be settled, particularly if it is large. Trying to treat everyone equally is very difficult when a family business or non-liquid assets like cottages or real estate are involved. Treating everyone fairly may not mean equally. These discussions should take place when you are there to explain the reasons for your decisions. Do not create a situation where the fighting starts over your coffin. That is not the legacy you want to leave.

Your kids also need to know your financial situation, especially if they might be called upon to help provide extra money, housing, or care. It is time we started talking about money with our kids as openly as Dr. Ruth talks about sex.

GIVING AWAY MONEY

How do you give your money away? This is not a question you asked back in Purple. Congratulations if you are in a position to consider how your estate should be distributed! There are some major issues you should consider before deciding where you want your assets to go and when:

- Are you sure you will have enough money to provide needed income and potential health care costs for yourself and your spouse for the balance of your lives? Unless you are sure, hang on to the money.
- Do you have the money set aside to pay any taxes due on your death?
- What charitable organizations do you want to support?
- Are your kids ready to receive any money they have not earned? Many a child has acquired insupportable lifestyle habits by receiving money from parents. You will remember back in White how a parent was a key person in teaching money values. Well, just because the kids are adults doesn't mean your responsibility declines. If your child makes $50,000 a year but because you give them $25,000 a year, he or she lives a lifestyle supportable by an income of $75,000, he or she is essentially on family welfare. What is he or she going to do when the gifts from you stop?
- Have you communicated your intentions clearly to your children? Doing so can reduce a lot of stress in family relations at the time of your death. Treating kids fairly and not necessarily equally is often necessary. Hearing it from you now is much better than from a lawyer later. This information must be in your will. It should include an itemized list of any personal possessions you want to go to specific people.

- Make sure the division of assets cannot be challenged under family and estate laws. You cannot leave everything to one child and nothing to a spouse or other children. Be aware that former spouses may be able to challenge your will. Get professional advice.
- Try to avoid using your money as a method of control. If you put your kids in the position of getting gifts if they suck up to you, and not if they don't, you have planted the seed of family discord. In the end this will not help the kids or family relations. Their respect for you will not be enhanced either.

TAXES ON GIFTS

Several issues should be considered in the disposition of your estate. These include reducing taxes, using trusts, and giving charitable gifts.

The first tax issue is attribution on gifts. Money given to a spouse that generates income will be taxable to you and not your spouse. Money given to a child or grandchild under eighteen will generate taxable income to you, except for capital gains, which are taxable to the child or grandchild. When the child or grandchild is over eighteen, income from gifts would not be attributable back to you.

PROBATE FEES

Probate fees are levied on your final estate. They used to be quite insignificant but in recent years provincial governments have increased them substantially to generate revenue. By naming beneficiaries on life insurance and RRSPs, these assets can bypass probate. Joint tenancy ownership and investing in segregated funds can also allow assets to bypass probate. Get your financial advisers to help with these issues.

CAPITAL GAINS TAX

Capital gains taxes are triggered on a distribution such as a sale or transfer of an asset. Your death is considered a deemed distribution. The transfer of an asset to a spouse can defer the tax, but eventually it will come due on your spouse's death or when the asset is disposed of. Seventy-five percent of this gain is added to your income, which can generate significant tax consequences. Assets like family cottages that have grown significantly in value may create a tax liability that will have to be met if the asset is going to remain in the family. Several strategies including life insurance and joint ownership exist to help alleviate this problem.

TAXES ON REAL ESTATE

Your principal residence is not subject to capital gains tax. In most provinces, your spouse has an interest in this home that is protected under family law. So you cannot give the home away without your spouse's agreement.

If you own assets in the United States such as a condominium or other property, these properties will be subject to U.S. estate taxes, which can be very high. If you have assets of this type, get professional advice about your tax liabilities. If you were born in the United States or have U.S. citizenship, you will also be liable for these estate taxes on your worldwide estate, even if you do not own property or have an income in the United States.

TRUSTS

Seek professional advice if you need to set up a trust. You may want to set up a trust to handle money for a minor or dependent child, to protect assets from creditors, or to allow your estate to be more privately and effectively settled. This is a vehicle more commonly used by the wealthy because of the setup and ongoing costs of a trust. However, it is something you may need to consider.

CHARITABLE GIFTS

Charitable organizations are being forced to be more creative and aggressive in seeking funds as governments continue to cut back. Universities, hospitals, museums, art galleries, and churches are only a few of the many organizations that are constantly seeking funds.

When I talked with a friend, Ian Fraser, who is a key fundraiser at Queen's University, he said that most of the university's largest individual donors are people who are in the Gold and Silver stages of their lives. This is no surprise. These people are now aware of how much money is likely to be necessary for themselves or their businesses, and how much can be gifted to organizations in which they have a strong belief. Ian and people like him can provide some very creative ways to help you package these gifts so that you receive some recognition today but the actual gift is paid out over time or at the time of your death. Charitable gifts are deductible from income; normally, the maximum is 75% of income, but up to 100% of income is now permitted in the year of your death. This creates some unique tax planning opportunities that may involve life insurance, or donations of securities, time, talent, or other types of property. It may involve the creation of a family foundation. The charities and your advisers will be delighted to give you assistance in setting up any planned gifts. Don't forget to inform your family of your plans.

THE CLUBHOUSE TURN

If we compare life to a horse race, you are coming around the clubhouse turn. You are heading down the final stretch. You can look back on career and ambition. You are loaded up with a will, a power of attorney, funeral arrangements, and trusts. You have done what you could for your kids, your grandkids, and even your favourite charities. You have arranged things so your friendly governments do not get more than is required in capital gains taxes and probate fees. Your own income is satisfactory and guaranteed for life. So you put your head down to make the final run to the finish while you are in Grey.

GREY
WITH A HELPING HAND

—

White starts with a slap on the butt. Grey is much the same, but it often starts with a kick in the butt. The kick is usually in the form of a significant change. This change could be to your health, your financial status, your relationships, or your accommodation. Change means learning, and learning means growth, so it is not time to pack up your tent yet. Life has a whole lot more lessons to teach us in Grey.

Grey may not seem to be a very attractive stage in life. It is true few would say it is the best. Some people will arrive in Grey far too early in life, as a result of poor health caused by bad luck or having lived a self-abusive lifestyle. Others may get there early and stay for quite a while because they have no money. Many will arrive because they have run out of purpose, or they despair over the loss of their loved ones and their friends. In short, they will have given up the will to live. Of course, some will arrive simply because of age. They gradually are less physically able to look after themselves and need some help.

In Silver we talked about a horse no longer going out on the range but choosing to stay in the corral. Well, in Grey, we stay inside or very close to the barn. And often it is not our choice.

Early in your life staying in the barn for a day would have been considered taking it easy. Today, all the days are like that. As always, you will have to adjust.

How you experience Grey may not be within your control. Everyone will have some dependency. Some will depend on a spouse who is still in Silver. Some will depend on children or other family members. Some will be in the hands of professional caregivers.

A few will have lost their mental abilities and may not be able to make decisions about the level of care they receive. Fortunately, this is a minority of people in Grey, but it is an important reason to have your personal affairs properly structured.

For the majority who do have their mental abilities, Grey may leave them feeling that a great deal of their independence is gone. They no longer have the freedom to drive, and their diet may be determined by others. Many other freedoms they once enjoyed may also be gone. However, if you are to learn the lessons Grey can teach, you must control the most important thing: your attitude.

ATTITUDE

Just because you are older does not mean you can't help others or teach others or love others. A whole lot of what you have learned in life can be shared or passed on.

The fastest percentage growth rate for any age group is the over–eighty-five-year-olds. This is a whole new frontier that is just beginning to be explored. Here are some thoughts of three centurions:

Jeanne Calment was a Frenchwoman who lived to the age of 122. Her doctors suggested she had good heredity and a healthy diet. She was born into a prosperous family and had enjoyed a leisured life. Her advice was to "keep smiling." She said, "I've lived so long because I have laughed a lot." Her comment in her 120s was that "I've only one wrinkle, and I'm sitting on it."

George Burns was a celebrated comedian and continued to perform to age one hundred. He believed a person should never retire. He said none of his friends who had retired were happy. The biggest difficulty he found with growing old was that all of his friends, including his beloved wife, Gracie, had gone. All those people with whom he had shared victories and defeats were gone, as well as the people with whom he had a common history. He felt isolated. Burns tried to overcome this through work and by openly flirting with young and attractive women.

This feeling of isolation was experienced by Marie Louise Meilleur, who was a Canadian and the world's oldest living person prior to her death at 117. She said, "I think God has forgotten me." One of her other philosophies was that "hard work never killed anyone."

The attitudes of people in Grey will be different than those experienced by a person in Purple. Their attitude can still be optimistic. However, people in Grey are fatalistic. Their theme song is: "Que sera sera — whatever will be, will be." Each one deals with his or her own sets of challenges and limitations. As in other stages, make sure your focus is on the world around you and not on yourself and the burdens you are being asked to carry.

Death is no longer feared; it is accepted. Everyone gets a turn. Those in Grey want to do more than just survive, they want to experience the simple joy of life. When that is gone — and each of us must establish that point for him or herself — they are willing to accept death. They do not want heroic medical efforts being made to prolong their discomfort. They want to be given the freedom to let go with dignity.

Their fatalistic attitude allows them to have a curiosity about what may come next. It also allows them to appreciate a simple moment or a warm relationship. The pressures of competition and image are gone. They may be even more willing to take risks. They have been able to attain a peace with themselves.

Grey is a time to make sense of your life. It is only at this point that all the experiences, all the memories, all the relationships blend together allowing you to see the whole picture. You no longer have to look in the rear-view mirror, but can stop, turn around, and look backwards over a lifetime, at your leisure. It is here that you can appreciate the risks you have taken, the challenges you have conquered, and the relationships you have enjoyed. It is a time to come to terms with the regrets you may have about your life or your relationships.

YOUR NEEDS

Your needs become very simple. They still involve the basics of food, clothes, and shelter. For some in Grey your needs are met in a facility designed for seniors. In this environment each individual's circumstances become similar. It is like high school where everyone was about the same age and at the same stage of life. Only this time you are old. These environments reduce the risk of your being isolated by providing you with many opportunities for social contact. A loving touch and a kind word are always appreciated. Even romance can still flourish in Grey.

People in Grey want to feel physically secure, they want access to private space, and they want opportunities to continue to learn and grow. Self-respect is essential to overall satisfaction with life. Paramount in maintaining this self-respect is having the ability to make your own choices. As long as you have the ability to choose, you should be allowed to do so. Well-meaning children should not try to push their own agenda onto their parents. The toughest decision you may have to make is to go against your parents' wishes for their own safety and well-being.

Let me say a few words to the adult child: You may now be the one in control; however, if the parent is not prepared to sell the house, do not force him or her. If your parents are not ready to go to a home or small accommodation, you have to wait. Yes, you can provide them with your opinion and information, but the decisions must be left to your parents as long as possible. I realize their decisions may not always be best for them, but this is one of those cruel twists of fate that allows parents to get even. You thought having your own kids should have been enough to even the score.

HEALTH CARE

This ability to choose should also not be taken away by the medical profession or by professional care providers. Every effort should be made to involve the senior. After all, it is their life and without their commitment, no prescription or treatment can provide the desired benefit.

In the future, home health care will continue to grow. It is being driven by the governments' desire to control costs. It is also being facilitated by breakthroughs in medical technology. Research also suggests that this is what the majority of people prefer. Home care will allow a senior to stay longer in a familiar environment. Families may be able to provide the necessary levels of support with the help of in-home professionals from time to time.

Society is going to have to learn how to deal with increasing numbers of people in Grey. The approach cannot be paternalistic, and it must involve seniors in the process. When the baby boomers arrive in Grey, their sheer numbers will swamp all the present facilities, but building more facilities is not going to be the answer. All individuals need to prepare for their tomorrow. This involves their attitudes, their knowledge, their fitness, their nutrition, and their personal financial resources.

MONEY

You should have done your financial planning prior to reaching Grey. By the time you reach this stage, you no longer want to have a day-to-day interest in money matters, but you do want to know that you have a regular income that can provide for your basic needs. Some people will have to limit themselves to what can be done on government pensions. Others will have company and personal pensions. The type of choices you can make will be limited if you do not have resources beyond the government programs. This is especially true for home care. The government will continue to offload this and many other health care costs to the individual. Even though some care options may be the ones you want, you don't want to have to put this cost burden on to your children. Hopefully, if you have followed the plans outlined in the other stages, you will be able to afford the necessary and desired level of care.

In addition, you should feel comfortable knowing that your funeral and estate plans have now been made. Your wishes have been communicated to the people who will have to deal with the relevant issues. You have set aside the financial resources to cover any costs. If you have not set aside resources, you may still qualify for a death benefit under the Canada Pension Plan. This death benefit is being reduced from approximately $3,560 to $2,500. War veterans may also qualify for funding of a funeral.

Make every effort to simplify your affairs. What may be a small effort for you today can save a lot of time and money later. You have made decisions that will help to minimize some potential estate taxes. These decisions may also expedite the matters of your estate and hopefully minimize any chance of family conflict. Try to have a reserve to cover unexpected costs. You have spent a lifetime building up your own little "pile" of money to whatever size, and just sitting on the "pile" may provide a real sense of security. If you have an emotional involvement with what your "pile" represents, do not just give the money to the kids so you can pay less in probate fees. Do not make minimizing the pension clawback your main focus. If you feel best just sitting on the money and paying the taxes, then do it. You have earned the right. Besides, the government needs the money, even if they don't always spend it wisely. As for your kids, they will just have to wait.

LOOKING BACK

Ultimately, a human can be active and productive for over a hundred years. Today, only one person in ten thousand reaches this age. This accomplishment is not purely hereditary, as no person who has lived to a hundred has had parents who lived to a hundred. Research suggests centenarians are people who have lived quiet, less ambitious lives. They are independent and satisfied with their choices in life. They appreciate the beauty of what life has to offer.

Whether you live to one hundred or not does not matter. What is important is that you have lived. You have followed your own drummer. You are satisfied when you look back over the many events and experiences you call your life.

This is when you give yourself the final test: "Has my life been worthwhile?" I told you earlier in a moment of philosophical outburst what I believed would be my criteria for answering this question. These were the love I had shared, the service I had given, and the teaching I had done.

You will need to develop your own criteria. When you have done that, and measured your life against them, I hope you like your answer.

Friends have suggested I create a final stage in the rainbow. It would be a one-line chapter containing the words "Fade to black."

I prefer to believe if we do meet our expectations on love, service, and teaching, then we do live on. For me the next colour should be more positive than Black. I think it should be something like Sunshine or Blue Sky. Those who are already in Grey know this best. Those of us on our way to Grey will learn.

SUMMARY

—

In mythology, the pot of gold is at the end of the rainbow. The combined result of the different colours that symbolize the stages of life is a rainbow of a different sort, a rainbow called life with each colour blending into the next. Throughout the book, I hope you have felt that life is a very exciting journey. Victories are there to be enjoyed during the journey. In short, life is in the living. It seemed a small leap to merge these topics into the title of this book, *The Gold Is in the Rainbow*.

Hopefully, in the reading you have learned some things. It has been a great learning experience for me to write the book. It has given me an opportunity to explore many of my own passions, to clarify and explain my own perspectives, to look into my own future.

It is all too clear that the book reeks of my personal bias. I do not ask you to agree with my opinions. I am only asking you to think. If you choose to have a different perspective, fine. Just be passionate about it. One of my greatest hopes is that in a small way this book will help stimulate some effective discussions about life and money between different generations. I encourage you to pass on the book to a parent or to a child. When they have read the section about themselves, try to have a conversation about it. This may help each of you in the process of learning and understanding.

I have tried to create a simple method for people to set priorities, but financial planning is required at each stage of life. Ultimately, you must become the master of your own money. Too many are victims of poor money management. Important decisions and events in life are missed because of a permanent state of financial crisis that deprives you of the freedom of choice. This is a freedom you should never be without. You do not want anyone else holding and playing your cards.

It is in making your own choices that you define yourself. This is what makes your life something unique. The words of the closing song in the movie *Pretty Woman* were:

"Everybody needs a dream,
Some dreams come true, some don't,
But keep on dreamin'."

This has been my own recurring theme, encouraging you to follow your passions, whether it is in education, adventure, romance, or your career. It is only in following these passions that you can approach your potential. Take the risks necessary so you do not end up summarizing your life with a whole lot of statements that begin with "if only." If your one life is going to make any difference to mankind, it will only be in those areas about which you can be truly passionate.

As you age, you will not think differently about yourself. You will always feel you are the same person, whether you are eighteen or eighty. The body changes, but the essentials of who you are do not. The older we are, the more aware we are of how short life really is. We are also more able to see our life as less of an individual adventure and more as a part of the ongoing community of mankind.

Old age and death are not to be feared. They are to be experienced. All of life's stages are to be fully experienced. We must live our lives in the way poet Dylan Thomas described:

> "Time held me green and dying
> Though I sang in my chains like the sea."

INDEX

—

accommodation, 43, 45, 78–79, 121,
   128
   for seniors, 167, 182–83
accounts, money market, 138
accounts, savings, 11–12, 22, 48,
   153
advisers
   financial, 49–50, 51, 67–69, 80,
      90–92, 94, 130, 133–36, 138,
      142, 152, 156, 169, 170, 174
   insurance, 101, 133–36
   investment, 136, 141
   tax, 132, 136, 140, 141
age, 96, 119, 157–58, 159–62, 179
allowances
   for children, 7–11
   for teenagers, 23–25
   retiring, 138
annuities, 148, 150–51
   conversion from RRIF, 150
   joint, 151, 152
   life, 150, 152, 155, 169
   mortality, 150–51
   prescribed, 155, 169
   term-certain, 150
assets, 97, 101, 137, 169, 170
   business, 65, 142–44
   division of, 173–74
   life insurance, 101
   liquidation of, 126, 153, 175

non-liquid, 172
   protection of, 133, 142, 175
automobile
   leasing, 43, 125, 126, 128, 153
   ownership, 28, 43, 63, 128, 153
averaging, dollar-cost, 74, 76

bankruptcy, 126
beneficiaries, 170, 174
benefits
   death, 101, 184
   employee, 51
   government, 129–30, 184. *See also*
      Old Age Security (OAS)
bequests, 173–74
bills, treasury, 93
blue-chip investments, 82–83, 84
bonds, 47, 80, 81, 86–87, 140, 153
Boom, Bust & Echo (Foot), 77–78
borrowing, 27, 61
   for RRSP, 74, 139–40
   from RRSP, 77, 79–80
Boyd, Dennis, 56
broker, discount, 90, 92
Brown, Robert, 147
budget planning, 46, 169
   for children, 9, 11
   for teenagers, 23–25, 28
Buffett, Warren, 92
Burns, George, 181

businesses
  accounting, 66, 68
  buying, 65–66, 111
  family, 26, 172
  goals, 67
  owning, 64–67, 132
  selling, 142–44, 155
  starting, 26, 38, 111
  succession plans, 171

Calment, Jeanne, 180
Canada Deposit Insurance Corp.
  (CDIC), 140
Canada Pension Plan (CPP), 50, 184
  death benefit, 184
Canada Savings Bonds, 47
Canadian investment, 82–84
Canadian Millennium Scholarships
  Foundation, 28
Canadian Snowbird Guide, The
  (Grey), 142
capital, 47, 48, 50, 61, 73, 102, 141,
  154, 169, 170
  in annuities, 155
  in RRIFs, 151
  tax-free, 103, 154
capital gain, 3, 71–72, 75, 82, 142,
  143, 144, 155
capital gains tax, 70, 97, 98, 102,
  142, 144, 154, 170, 174, 175
  deferred, 98, 144
cars. See automobile
careers
  change, 112–13
  opportunities, 18, 32, 35–37
  planning, 17–19, 22, 25, 35–40, 54
  second, 111, 131, 132, 137
cash
  lump-sum payment, 138–39
  sources of, 153–54
  withdrawal from RRSP, 151
charitable bequests, 173, 176
children
  adult, 113–14, 123, 159, 164, 172,
    173, 180, 182–83
  allowances, 7–11, 23–25
  bequest to, 173
  education costs, 3–4, 27–29, 81, 97,
    99

gifts to, 173, 174
learning to budget, 9, 11
and money, 2–13
and savings, 11–13
teenaged, 15–30
trusts for, 175–76
clawback, pension, 145–46, 152–53,
  185
compound interest, 5, 12, 49, 73, 86,
  131
  "Rule of 72," 12, 49, 77, 93, 129
computer programs, 11, 46, 70, 137
contract employment, 67
cost of living, 32, 138
cottages, family, 122, 142, 153, 171,
  172, 175
credit cards, 10, 28, 42, 101, 125,
  126, 127
credit, lines of, 126
creditors, 101, 126, 175

death
  benefits, 101, 184
  of spouse, 120, 133, 170
  taxes due on, 102, 151, 170, 175
debt, 60–61, 74, 102, 105, 125–29,
  154
  freedom from, 124, 153
  non-deductible, 76
  reduction, 42, 139–40, 141
  and young people, 27–29
deferred capital gains, 98, 175
Deferred Profit Sharing Plans (DPSPs),
  139, 170
deferred taxes, 48–49
defined benefit plans, 147
defined contribution plans, 147
disability insurance, 50–51, 102, 103,
  126, 133
discount brokers, 90, 92
dismissal, wrongful, 138
diversified investment portfolios, 81,
  82, 87–88, 140–41, 150
dividend funds, 83
dividend income, 3, 71–72, 83, 97, 144
division of assets, 173–74
divorce, 56, 58–59, 120, 133, 170, 174
dollar-cost averaging, 74, 76
Dominguez, Joe, 60

downsizing
  corporate, 105, 126, 138
  personal, 128, 141
education
  continuing, 79–80, 115, 117, 118,
    121
  cost of, 3–4, 27–29, 81, 97, 102,
    158
  financial assistance for, 28
  funds, 3–6, 99
  planning, 17–18, 22
  using RRSPs to pay for, 79–80
employee benefits, 51
employment, 108–9, 166
  finding, 25–26, 37
  flextime, 110, 129
  insurance, 126
  loss of, 102–3, 124, 126, 138
  part-time, 110, 129, 137
  scaling down, 109, 129, 162–63
  self-, 67, 121, 132
  for seniors, 162–63, 166
  trends, 67, 68, 102–3
entrepreneurs, 63–67, 111
equity investments, 74, 82, 140
estate
  law, 174
  planning, 97, 100–101, 132, 136,
    151, 170–76, 184
  taxes, 142, 170, 175, 185
executors, 69–70, 133, 170
expenses
  management, 42–46, 127, 169
  tracking, 11, 46, 96, 134, 137

family, 22, 32, 53, 54, 56–59
  financial assistance from, 23–24
  foundation, 176
family law, 59, 101, 174, 175
financial advisers. See advisers
financial styles
  entrepreneurs, 63–67
  gamblers, 64
  savers, 62–63
  spenders, 60–62, 64
financing
  businesses, 65, 143
  homes, 78

fixed income funds, 82
flextime employment, 110, 129
food expenses, 28, 43, 44, 45, 127
Foot, David, 77–78
foreign investment, 75, 83–84, 88,
    140
Foster, Sandra, 172
foundation, family, 176
Fraser, Ian, 176
funds
  education, 3–6
  fixed income, 82
  growth, 3, 83–84
  long-term, 3
  segregated, 174
funds, mutual. See mutual funds
funeral planning, 133, 170, 184

gifts, 174, 176
  to children, 9, 173, 174
  planned, 176
global funds, 83
goal-setting, 125
  financial, 91–92, 96, 101
  personal, 22, 47, 67, 108
Goodman, Ron, 40
government benefits, 129–30, 145–47,
    162–63, 169, 184
  Canada Pension Plan, 50, 184
  clawback of, 145–46, 152–53, 185
  Guaranteed Income Supplement,
    145–46, 154
  Old Age Security, 130, 145–46, 152
  Seniors Benefit (repealed), 146
grandchildren, 121, 123
grandparents, 58, 109, 110, 114, 118,
    121, 123, 159
  as source of education funds, 5–6,
    99
Grey, Douglas, 142
grief and grieving, 165–66
grocery shopping. See food expenses
group insurance, 51, 102–103, 133–36
growth funds, 3, 83–84
Guaranteed Income Supplement (GIS),
    145–46, 154
Guaranteed Investment Certificates
    (GIC), 89–90, 140
Gurney, Kathleen, 60

Hartman, George, 85
health, 20, 22, 53–56, 103, 106, 118,
    119–20, 123, 125, 126, 133, 145,
    151
  care, 21, 130, 183–84
  costs, 122, 130, 173
  emotional, 168–69
  home care, 183–84
  insurance outside Canada, 130
  in old age, 157–58, 159, 164, 166,
    168–69, 173, 179
  power of attorney, 171
heirs, 151, 170
hobbies, 45, 56, 109, 117–18, 125,
    166, 169
Hobbs, Whit, 41
homes
  downsizing, 141, 153
  mortgage, 77, 153
  ownership, 76–79, 97, 121, 128,
    141, 153–54
  refinancing, 153
  relocation, 120–23, 128, 141,
    163–64, 167
  rental, 128
  reverse mortgages, 154
  selling, 153, 155
Home Buyers Plan, 77

incentive packages, retirement, 137
income
  dividend, 3, 71–72, 83, 97, 144
  earned, 137, 144
  fixed, 150
  interest, 3, 71–72, 75, 82, 97, 98,
    138, 144, 154, 155
  investment, 128, 143
  rental, 98, 142, 144
  seniors', 184
  taxable, 73
  U.S., 142
income tax, 3, 5, 46, 47, 70–72, 73,
    138, 139, 148, 151, 155
  deferred, 3, 48–49, 72–76
  minimizing, 142–44, 153
  refund, 79
  and RRIFs, 148–50
  software, 70
income-splitting, 70, 138, 153

inflation, 102, 129–30, 131, 137,
    140, 151
  effect on government benefits, 146
  protection from, 136
inheritances, 74, 100–101, 105, 140,
    153, 172
insurance, 50–51, 102–103, 133,
    136
  advisers, 136
  disability, 50–51, 102, 103, 133
  employment, 126
  group, 51, 102–103, 133–36
  health, 130
  life. See life insurance
  mortgage, 102
interest
  compound, 5, 12, 49, 73, 86, 131
    See also "Rule of 72"
  income, 3, 71–72, 75, 82, 97, 98,
    138, 144, 154, 155
  non-deductible, 78, 101, 125, 140
  tax-deductible, 125, 154
international investments, 75, 83–84,
    88, 140
Internet, 6, 12, 56, 92
in-trust accounts, 3, 4, 70, 99
investments, 47, 53, 61, 72, 73,
    80–100, 101, 137
  advisers, 136, 14
  blue-chip, 82–83, 84
  bonds, 80, 81, 140, 153
  brokers, discount, 90, 92
  Canadian, 82–84
  diversification of, 81, 82, 87–88,
    140–41, 150
  equity, 74, 82, 140
  foreign, 75, 83–84, 88, 140
  GICs, 89–90, 140, 154
  income, 128, 143
  liquidity, 82, 99–100, 141, 153
  mortgages, 82, 140
  mutual funds, 81–85, 153
  planning, 80–100, 140–41
  portfolio, 75, 80–100, 140–41, 150
  real estate, 75, 80, 81, 84, 97,
    99–100, 140–41
  risk in, 53, 61, 80–89, 91, 94,
    96–98, 140–41, 150
  RRIFs, 150

RRSPs. *See* Registered Retirement
Savings Plans
stocks, 80, 81, 153
T-bills, 93–94

Jacks, Evelyn, 71
jobs. *See* employment
joint annuities, 151, 152
joint ownership, 175
joint tenancy, 171, 174

law, family, 59, 101
leases, automobile, 43, 125, 126, 128,
153
leisure, 107, 108, 115–19, 127
life annuities, 150, 152, 155
life expectancy, 96, 119, 141
Life Income Funds (LIFs), 148, 152,
170
life insurance, 50–51, 101, 102–3,
126, 133, 153, 154, 176
as collateral, 154
as education savings plan, 5, 102
in estate planning, 50, 101, 170,
174, 175, 176
permanent, 50, 101, 133
term, 50, 102, 133
life partners. *See* partners, life
life planning, 31–41, 120–23
lines of credit, 126
liquidation of assets, 126
liquidity
of capital, 103
of investment, 82, 99–100
loans
assets as collateral for, 65
to children, 9
collateral, 65, 126
consolidation, 3
education, 28, 29
non-deductible interest, 101
Locked-In Retirement Accounts
(LIRAs), 152
longevity, 96, 119, 141
lump-sum payments, 138–39, 155

market, stock, 87, 90, 92–94
marriage, 56–59, 101, 120, 170
Meals on Wheels, 164

medical costs, 51, 97
Meilleur, Marie Louise, 181
mentoring, 35, 114–15
money management, 23, 42–46, 81,
188
and teenagers, 23–25, 27–29
money market accounts, 138
money market funds, 82
money purchase pension plans, 147
Morgan, J. P., 80–81
mortality, 150–51
mortgages, 47, 77, 78–79, 101, 102,
125, 128
foreclosure, 126
funds, 82, 140–41
payments, 78–79
reverse, 154, 169
mutual funds, 3, 12–13, 22, 47,
81–85, 98, 99, 144, 153, 169
blue-chip, 82–84
dividend, 83
equity, 82
fixed income, 82
global, 83
growth, 3, 83–84
money-market, 82
mortgage, 82, 140–41
specialty, 84
systematic withdrawal, 155, 169

National Council on Welfare, 146
National Forum on Health, 124
net-worth statements, 96, 134–36
non-resident aliens (in U.S.), 142

old age, 159–62
needs in, 182–83
See also seniors
Old Age Security (OAS), 130, 145–47,
152, 169, 184
clawback, 145–46, 152–53, 185
ownership, joint, 175

parents, 56–59, 109
and cost of education, 99
teaching children about money, 2–13
and teenagers, 16, 18, 21, 23–25
partners, life, 32, 33–34, 50, 54,
56–59, 70, 74–75. *See also* spouses

part-time employment, 110, 137
payments, lump-sum, 138–39
pensions, 49, 97, 126, 131, 136, 137,
    139, 145–48, 151–52, 169, 184
  beneficiaries, 170
  Canada Pension Plan, 50, 145, 184
  clawback, 145–46, 152–53, 185
  defined benefits, 147
  defined contributions, 147
  government, 50, 129, 130,
    145–47,152, 162–63, 169, 184
  Locked-In Retirement Accounts
    (LIRAs), 152
  money purchases, 147
  Old Age Security, 130, 145–47, 152,
    169, 184
  planning, 47, 96–97
  RRSPs. See Registered Retirement
    Savings Plans
permanent life insurance, 51, 101,
    133
  conversion from term life insurance,
    133
planned gifts, 176
planners, financial, 49–50, 51, 67–69,
    80, 90–92, 94, 97–98, 137, 169
portfolio of investments, 75, 80–100,
    140–41, 150
  diversification of, 81, 82, 87–88,
    140–41, 150
power of attorney, 70, 132, 133, 171
prescribed annuities, 155, 169
principal residences, 76, 142, 175
probate fees, 101, 132, 170, 174, 185
programs, computer, 11, 46, 70, 137
property
  recreational, 100, 122, 141, 142,
    153, 172, 175
  rental, 154
  sale of, 155, 175

Queen's University, 176
Quicken, 11

rates of return, 47, 48, 69, 93
real estate
  commercial, 99
  home ownership, 76–79, 97, 142,
    171, 175

  investing in, 75, 78, 80, 81, 90, 97,
    98, 99–100, 140–41
  recreational property, 100, 122, 141,
    142, 153, 172, 175
rear-view mirror thinking, 19, 22, 36,
    41, 112, 156, 159
recreation, 121, 158
recreational vehicles (RVs), 122, 123,
    153
refinancing, 153, 154
refunds, tax, 79
Registered Education Savings Plans
    (RESPs), 4–5, 99
  transfer of funds from, 5
Registered Retirement Income Funds
    (RRIFs), 148–50, 151, 169, 170
  conversion to annuity, 150
  and spouse, 149–50
  trustees, 148–49
Registered Retirement Savings Plans
    (RRSPs), 5, 48–50, 70, 72–76, 83,
    97, 101, 102, 105, 128, 131, 137,
    139–41, 147–48, 150, 169, 170
  beneficiaries, 170, 174
  borrowing for, 74, 125, 139–40
  borrowing from, 77, 79–80
  contributions to, 138, 139, 141, 144
  and deferred tax, 72–76
  foreign content of, 75, 88
  Home Buyers Plan, 77
  with life insurance company, 126
  locked-in, 151–52
  options for use of, 148–52
  rollover from retiring allowance,
    138–39
  seizure of, 126
  spousal, 74–75, 101, 138, 149
  tax refunds from, 79
  transfer from RESPs to, 5
  withdrawal from, 139, 151
relocation, 120–23, 163–64, 167
remarriage, 101, 170
rental
  accommodation, 128, 153
  income, 98, 142, 144
  property, 154
residence
  outside Canada, 141–42
  principal, 76, 142, 175

retirement, 49, 106, 115
  allowances, 138
  communities, 121, 122
  early, 131–32
  incentive packages, 137
  need for routine in, 109–15, 125
  planning for, 56, 81, 96–97, 120–23,
    124, 130, 134–35, 136–38, 140
  semi-retirement, 109
  temporary, 110–11
  trial, 129
retiring allowance formula, 138
Revenue Canada, 3, 5, 71, 73, 126
reverse mortgages, 154, 169
risk
  capital, 80
  in investment, 61, 80–89, 91, 94,
    96–98, 140–41, 150
  management of, 53, 85–89
  personal, 111
Risk Is a Four Letter Word
  (Hartman), 85
Robin, Vicki, 60
rollover of retiring allowance to
  RRSPs, 138–39
"Rule of 72," 12, 49, 77, 93, 129
Russell, Bertrand, 29

sabbatical, 111, 129
Savage, John, 47–48
savers, 62–63
saving, 46–50, 53, 73
  programs for children, 11–13
  for retirement, 137
  and teenagers, 21–23
savings
  accounts, 11–12, 22, 153
  spending in retirement, 136
scholarships, 28
security
  economic, for seniors, 147
  occupational, 114
  in old age, 145–47, 152, 182, 185
segregated funds, 174
self-assessment, 35
self-employment, 67, 102–3, 121,
  132
self-promotion, 25–26, 37
selling a business, 66, 142–44

seniors
  centres for, 164, 169
  estate planning for, 170
  and family, 159, 164, 167, 180, 185
  health of, 157–58, 159, 164, 166,
    168–69, 173, 179
  housing for, 167–76, 182
  and independence, 180, 182
  and loneliness, 163–65, 179, 181
  low-income, 46
  mental capacity of, 160, 180
  needs of, 182–83
  and personal growth, 161–62
  security of, 147
  and sex, 160
  and work, 162–63
Seniors Benefit, 146
service clubs, 116
severance payments, 74, 105, 138–39
Shaw, George Bernard, 34
significant others. See partners, life;
  spouses
small-cap stocks, 93–94
smoking, 28, 43, 55, 168
snowbirds, 122, 141–42, 153, 163
software, financial, 11, 46, 70, 137
spenders, 60–62, 64
sports, 19–20, 45, 117
spousal RRSPs, 74–75, 101, 138,
  149
spousal trusts, 70
spouses, 50, 54, 56–59, 70, 74, 128,
  133, 175, 180
  and annuities, 151, 152
  as beneficiaries, 170
  gifts to, 174
  health concerns about, 158, 173
  income-splitting with, 70, 138
  and LIFs, 152
  loss of, 120, 133, 165–66
  and RRIFs, 149–50
Stanley, Thomas, 63
stocks, 80, 81, 87, 98, 153
  common, 12
  foreign, 87–88
  market, 87, 90, 92–94
  small-cap, 93–94
student debt, 27–29
succession plans, business, 171

summer cottages, 122, 142, 153, 171, 172, 175
systematic withdrawal plans, 155–56, 169

tax
  advisers, 132, 136, 140, 141
  audits, 71
  havens, 123
  planning, 70, 71, 80, 136, 176
  shelters, 98
taxable gains, 79
taxable income, 73
taxes, 63, 97, 98, 132, 140
  business, 68
  capital gains, 70, 97, 98, 102, 142, 154
  due on death, 133, 170, 173
  estate, 142, 170, 175, 185
  income. *See* income tax
teenagers and young adults, 15–30
  and adventure, 20–21, 22
  and athletics, 19–20
  career planning for, 17–19, 22, 25
  car ownership by, 28
  and debt, 27–29
  and education, 17–18, 22, 27–29
  goal-setting for, 22–23
  and money management, 23–25, 27–29
  and parents, 16, 18, 21, 23–25
  part-time jobs for, 16, 25–26, 28
  and romance, 21–23
  and savings, 22–23
  and travel, 20–21, 22
tenancy, joint, 171, 174
term life insurance, 51, 102, 133
  conversion to permanent life insurance, 133
term-certain annuities, 150
termination of employment, 138
tin-can theory, 47–48
Toronto Stock Exchange, 87, 144
travel, 20–21, 22, 56, 110, 116–17, 123
treasury bills (T-bills), 93–94
trusts, 175–76
  account, 3, 4

  educational, 101
  spousal, 70
trustees, RRIF, 148–49

unemployment, 102–103, 124, 126
United States
  assets in, 170, 175
  citizenship, 175
  estate taxes, 170, 175
  income, 142
  old age security, 147
  residence in, 141–42
  taxes, 142, 170

vacation, 28, 45, 100, 109, 129
  property, 100, 122, 141
values, financial, 59–67
  entrepreneurs, 63–67
  savers, 62–63
  spenders, 60–62, 64
values, personal, 61–62, 105
veterans' benefits, 184
volunteering, 56, 109, 116–18, 164

Wall Street (film), 86
Wal-Mart, 163
weddings, 45–46
widowhood, 165–66
wills, 68, 69–70, 100, 101, 132, 133, 150, 170, 173
  probate fees, 101, 132, 170, 174, 185
windfalls, 140
withdrawal plans, systematic, 155–56, 169
withholding taxes, 138–39
work. *See* employment
workaholism, 105, 108, 123
wrongful dismissal, 138

Yeats, W. B., 107
You Can't Take It With You (Foster), 172
young people, 15–30. *See also* teenagers
Your Money or Your Life (Dominguez and Robin), 60, 61
Your Money Personality (Gurney), 60